Royal QUIZ

Richard Garrett

Longman

Longman Group Limited,
Longman House, Burnt Mill, Harlow,
Essex CM20 2JE, England
and Associated Companies throughout the world.

© Longman Group Limited 1985

First published 1985

British Library Cataloguing in Publication Data
Garrett, Richard
    Royal quiz.—(Longman quiz books)
    1. Royal houses—Great Britain—Miscellanea
    I. Title
    941′.009′92   DA28.1

    ISBN 0-582-89264-3

Set in 10/11 pt and 8/8 pt 'Monophoto' Apollo
by Chambers Wallace Ltd, London
Printed in Great Britain
by Spottiswoode Ballantyne, Colchester and London

Contents

Introduction   v
Royalty and their relatives   1
The homes of Kings and
  Queens   3
Royalty and war   5
Coronations   7
Royalty and marriage   9
Royalty as trend-setters   11
Who said?   13
Royalty and death   15
Royalty and regalia   17
Royal Yachts   19
Royal idiosyncrasies   21
Royal bodyguards   23
The Royal Household   25
Royal addresses   27
Other titles   29
Which regiment?   31
Royal babies   33
Royal hobbies   35
Royalty and horses   37
Royalty and their pets   39
Who are (or were)?   41
Ceremonial matters   43
Royal visits   45
Medals and decorations   47
Royal finances   49
Royal shopping   51
The name game   53
Royal ancestors   55
Royalty and charity   57
Royalty and railways   59
A batch of bloomers   61
Royal customs   63

Royal servants   65
Royalty and the media   67
Royalty in and out of
  danger   69
Royal birthdays   71
Innovations   73
Royal etiquette   75
Who said?   77
Royalty and showbiz   79
Royalty and cars   81
Royalty and books   83
Royalty and sport   85
Royalty and aeroplanes   87
Royalty and politics   89
Royalty and holidays   91
Royalty and education   93
The reigns of Kings and
  Queens   95
Royalty in sickness and
  in health   97
Friends and connections   99
Maiden names   101
Royalty and music   103
Who said?   105
Royalty and the Empire   107
Animals presented to
  Royalty   109
Royal routine   111
Royal pomp and
  heraldry   113
Royal monuments   115
Succession and
  precedence   117
When?   119

Other books in the series

Book Quiz
Word Quiz
Britain Now Quiz
Film Quiz
Word Teaser

Introduction

MANY YEARS AGO, a leading national newspaper published a regular feature entitled 'It's Fun Finding Out'. Whilst there has been no conscious attempt to make the questions in this book particularly difficult (and certainly none to make them too easy), there will no doubt be many that even the most alert Royalty watcher cannot answer.

I make no apologies for these. 'It's Fun Finding Out' has its quiz equivalent in most of the newspapers round about Christmas time. To be able to answer a quite modest proportion of their questions may be considered an achievement. Nevertheless, they lose little of their appeal for this. A great deal of the pleasure comes from looking up the solutions.

A quiz, indeed, is more than a test of knowledge: it is an amusing way of adding to one's stock of information. Most of it, of course, is useless and it is none the worse for that. It may be an advantage to be well versed in more practical matters, but there is also a place for those quaint little fragments of learning that cause one to exclaim 'Well I never!', or 'Did you know?' Without them life – and history in particular – would be very dull.

Most of the questions in this book belong to a period of British Royal history that began with the birth of Queen Victoria. However, the ancestry of the Royal Family can be traced back to William I – and beyond. Thus it would be wrong to exclude the more distant past, which is, after all, part of the Royal fabric. Consequently, there are several exceptions to what is no more than a very rough and ready rule.

Many people helped me to compile this book; but I should like to thank particularly my wife and daughter for their suggestions and advice, Betty Jenner who typed the manuscript, the reference librarian of Tunbridge Wells Public Library, and the innumerable authors who, apparently dedicated to searching for the secrets of Royalty, contributed so much to my research.

Richard Garrett

Royalty and their relatives

1 Which Queen's aunt by marriage was denied Royal status?

2 Which member of the Royal Family is distantly related to a popular novelist?

3 Which King married his sister-in-law?

4 Which Royal referred to whom as his 'honorary' grandfather?

5 Whose eldest son was alleged (wrongly, no doubt) to have been friendly with Jack the Ripper?

6 Which Queen ordered the execution of her successor's mother?

7 Which Queen's eldest child became the mother of one of her country's most hated enemies?

8 Which Sovereign had five children: two of which succeeded to the British throne, and one who became father of a British Monarch?

9 Which Sovereign was illegitimate by birth?

10 Who was the father of the first Prince of Wales?

11 Which Sovereign's cousin became famous in the world of opera?

12 Which Royal's mother opened a shop in Paris?

13 How many grandchildren does Queen Elizabeth the Queen Mother have – and which Royal widow refused to be called 'Queen Mother'?

14 One (and only one) British Monarch belonged to the House of Saxe-Coburg. Who?

15 Which Sovereign in this century had a son who died at the age of fourteen?

1   Queen Elizabeth II. Her uncle, briefly Edward VIII, married Wallis Simpson – an American divorcee. As such, she could not become Queen; nor – though she became Duchess of Windsor – was she accorded the status of Royal Duchess (in other words, she could not be addressed as 'Your Royal Highness').

2   The Princess of Wales. Her stepgrandmother is Barbara Cartland, writer of romantic fiction.

3   King Henry VIII. His first wife was Catherine of Aragon, widow of his deceased elder brother, Prince Arthur.

4   Prince Charles referred to his great uncle, the late Earl Mountbatten, as his 'honorary' grandfather.

5   Malicious gossip alleged that the Duke of Clarence, eldest son of Edward VII, was in some way connected with Jack the Ripper. The Duke ('Eddy' as he was called) died of pneumonia in 1892, and the succession passed to the Duke of York – later King George V.

6   Elizabeth I ordered the execution of Mary Queen of Scots – the mother of James VI of Scotland. On her deathbed, Elizabeth named James as her successor. Thus he became James I of England.

7   Queen Victoria's eldest child, Victoria, Princess Royal, married Frederick III of Prussia – and thus became the mother of Kaiser Wilhelm II, who was held responsible for the outbreak of the First World War.

8   Two of George III's sons succeeded to the throne, and became George IV and William IV. His fourth son, Edward, Duke of Kent, was the father of Queen Victoria.

9   William I was the illegitimate son of Robert, Duke of Normandy. His mother was the daughter of a wealthy tanner. During his lifetime, many writers referred to him as William the Bastard.

10   Edward I was staying at Caernarvon in 1284, when his first son (later Edward II) was born. With grim humour, he told the Welsh leaders that he would give them a prince who 'could not speak a word of English'. In 1301, the lad – now a teenager – was invested as Prince of Wales.

11   Queen Elizabeth II's cousin, the Earl of Harewood, has been managing director of the English National Opera since 1972.

12   Prince Philip's mother, Princess Alice, opened a shop in Paris and donated the profits to penniless Greek refugees.

13   Queen Elizabeth the Queen Mother has six grandchildren: Prince Charles, Princess Anne, Prince Andrew, and Prince Edward – and Princess Margaret's David, Viscount Linley, and Lady Sarah Armstrong-Jones. Queen Mary objected to being referred to as the Queen Mother after the death of her husband, George V.

14   Edward VII was the only English Sovereign to belong to the house of Saxe-Coburg. His father was Prince Albert of Saxe-Coburg and Gotha. His successor, George V, was the first of the House of Windsor.

15   The youngest son of King George V and Queen Mary was Prince John, who was born in 1905 and died in 1919. The Prince was an epileptic – an illness that, in those days, could not be controlled by drugs.

The homes of Kings and Queens

1 What former Royal home used to contain an observatory and a menagerie?

2 What famous London landmark was once the gateway to a palace?

3 What Royal home had a miniature Swiss chalet in its grounds?

4 Who purchased Sandringham – and for how much?

5 Windsor Castle is the oldest of today's Royal residences. Who built the original castle?

6 Clarence House in London is the home of the Queen Mother. Which King lived in it because he preferred it to Buckingham Palace? And who was 'Clarence'?

7 When was Buckingham Palace acquired as the London home of the reigning Monarch?

8 Which Royal owned a ranch in Canada?

9 What is the official home of the Sovereign in Scotland?

10 Who bought a castle on the northernmost tip of Scotland – and, thereby, acquired a resident ghost?

11 Balmoral cost Queen Victoria and Prince Albert £31,500. How did they acquire the money?

12 Shortly after one Royal home had been purchased, it was burned down. Which?

13 Hampton Court was once a Royal palace. Who abandoned it?

14 Which Royal home is now part of a museum?

15 The Brighton Pavilion was built by George IV for his unlawful wife, Mrs Maria Fitzherbert. Who owns it now?

Answers The homes of Kings and Queens

1   The Tower of London. It once contained a menagerie, an observatory – also a mint and a resident bowmaker.

2   Marble Arch was originally the main gateway to Buckingham Palace. It was moved to its present site in 1851 on the orders of Queen Victoria.

3   The Swiss Cottage, as it was called, was erected at Osborne on the Isle of Wight at the instigation of Prince Albert. It was equipped with kitchen utensils and tools, so that the elder children should learn how to cook and become proficient at carpentry. The prefabricated units were imported from the Continent.

4   Sandringham was bought by Edward VII (when Prince of Wales) in 1862 (a few months before his marriage). He paid £22,000 for the estate, which then covered 7,000 acres.

5   The site of Windsor Castle was chosen by William I for its strategic value. Upon it, he built a fortress to command the approaches to London. Henry II began work on the stone buildings (including the famous Round Tower) in 1165. The task took six years to complete.

6   Clarence House was occupied by William IV shortly after he came to the throne. Like a number of other Sovereigns, he did not care for Buckingham Palace. An overhead corridor was built, connecting it to St James's Palace, where he conducted his official business. Its name is derived from the Duke of Clarence – the King's title before his accession.

7   Buckingham Palace was originally Buckingham House – the London home of the Duke of Buckingham built on land given to him by Queen Anne. George III bought it in 1762. The present frontage was constructed in 1911.

8   Edward VIII (then Prince of Wales) bought a 4,000-acre ranch 40 miles south of Calgary, Canada, in 1919. It was to be an 'escape from the sometimes too-confining, too-well-ordered, island life of Britain'.

9   Holyrood House in Edinburgh.

10   The Queen Mother bought Castle Mey overlooking the Pentland Firth. The ghost is Lady Fanny Sinclair. She threw herself from a window in the tower – where she was held captive after trying to elope with a servant.

11   Balmoral was bought by Queen Victoria from a legacy of £$\frac{1}{4}$ million, which was bequeathed to her by an eccentric admirer named John Camden Neild.

12   Kensington Palace, formerly Nottingham House, was bought by William III. Shortly after he acquired it, the building burned down and Sir Christopher Wren was commissioned to restore it.

13   George III abandoned Hampton Court (preferring Buckingham Palace) – though it still belongs to the Crown. It has been open to the public since the days of Queen Victoria.

14   The Queen's House, built by James I for his wife, Anne of Denmark, is now part of the National Maritime Museum at Greenwich.

15   Queen Victoria sold the Brighton Pavilion to the local corporation.

Royalty and war

1   Which was the last King to lead his troops in battle?

2   Which Royal served in a gun turret during the Battle of Jutland?

3   In which warship did Prince Andrew serve in the Falklands campaign, and what were his duties?

4   Which Royal flew over the front line in the First World War?

5   Which Royal was killed on active service in the Second World War?

6   The frigate HMS *Magpie* was commanded by a member of the Royal Family. Who?

7   Which Royal was responsible for defeating the Highlanders at the Battle of Culloden?

8   Which Sovereign introduced an entirely new concept of fighting battles?

9   Which of the present Queen's relations was interned in Colditz during the Second World War?

10   Which King was responsible for killing his prisoners during what battle?

11   Which King could take the credit for winning a naval battle?

12   Which member of the Royal Family served in the ATS during the Second World War?

13   Who is said to have been pleased when Buckingham Palace was bombed in September 1940?

1   George II took command of the British troops at the Battle of Dettingen in 1743. James Wolfe (later General Wolfe who captured Quebec) wrote that 'The King was in the midst of the fight'.

2   The Duke of York (later George VI) was a midshipman at the Battle of Jutland. He served in a gun turret aboard the battleship HMS *Collingwood*. Later he was posted to the Royal Naval Air Service at Cranwell.

3   During the Falklands campaign, Prince Andrew served in the aircraft carrier HMS *Invincible* as a pilot of a Wessex helicopter.

4   The Prince of Wales (later Edward VIII) was taken on a flight just before the battle of the Somme in 1916. 'I don't think I was scared,' he said. 'It was just a new experience.'

5   HRH the Duke of Kent was killed in 1942, when a Sunderland flying boat in which he was travelling crashed into a hill in the Highlands. The Duke was serving in the RAF's welfare branch. He was on his way from Scotland to Reykjavik when the disaster occurred.

6   Prince Philip, who served with the Royal Navy throughout the Second World War, commanded HMS *Magpie*. It was his last ship, and there is a model of it in his study on the Royal Yacht.

7   George II's son defeated Prince Charles Stewart's followers at the Battle of Culloden. Afterwards, his behaviour to the defeated clansmen was so atrocious, that he was nicknamed 'The Butcher'.

8   At the Battle of Hastings, the Duke of Normandy adopted tactics that can be compared to present day warfare. First he softened up the enemy by a volley of arrows from his archers (comparable, perhaps, to an artillery barrage). Then he sent in his infantry to cut holes in their ranks. Finally, the cavalry penetrated the gaps and attacked from the rear (as tanks might do).

9   The Earl of Harewood was taken prisoner when serving with the Grenadier Guards in 1944. He was moved to Colditz with other POWs related to VIPs – probably to be used as a hostage.

10   King Henry V slew many of his prisoners during the Battle of Agincourt. The King had misread the situation; and, fearing that they might attack him from the rear, ordered the captives to be put to the sword. However, he insisted that the nobility should be spared (presumably because they commanded larger ransoms).

11   Edward III commanded the English fleet that fought the French at the Battle of Sluys in 1340. The French vessels were almost entirely destroyed with considerable casualties. Edward is said to have been wounded.

12   Then Princess Elizabeth, the Queen served in the ATS during the Second World War. Her number was 230873; her rank was that of second subaltern; and she was described as Elizabeth Alexandra Mary Windsor – aged 18, with blue eyes, brown hair, and 5ft 3ins tall. She learned how to read a map, maintain vehicles, and to drive through London's traffic.

13   After Buckingham Palace was bombed on 13 September 1940, the Queen (now the Queen Mother) is reputed to have said, 'I'm glad we've been bombed. It makes me feel that I can look the East End in the face'.

Coronations

1 At whose coronation did a peer of the realm trip over his gown on the steps leading to the throne?

2 What Sovereign was crowned twice in the UK?

3 At whose coronation did an onlooker refer to a visiting Queen's diminutive companion as 'her lunch'?

4 Whose was the first coronation to be televised?

5 What coach is used by the Sovereign at the coronation?

6 Whose coronation had to be postponed because of illness?

7 Who described his journey to Westminster Abbey as 'one of the most uncomfortable rides I have ever had in my life'?

8 At whose coronation did free wine flow from the fountains of London?

9 At whose coronations did special tube trains convey peers and MPs to Westminster?

10 Who is responsible for organizing coronations?

11 Which King refused to allow his Queen to attend his coronation?

12 At whose coronation did a number of peers refuse to attend – on the grounds that they were not prepared to pay for their robes?

13 At whose coronation did local residents complain about the rowdiness of the Royal celebrations following the ceremony?

14 Who used to ride on horseback into the room where the ceremony was taking place?

15 What part does a team of shire horses, loaned by a well-known brewer, play in the coronation?

Answers Coronations

1 The 82-year-old Lord Rolle tripped over his gown and fell as he approached the throne at the coronation of Queen Victoria.

2 King Charles II had two coronations. The first was a secret ceremony at Scone in Scotland. The second was at Westminster after the Restoration. At the former, the Scottish clergy refused to carry out the ceremony of annointment by oil.

3 At the coronation of Queen Elizabeth II, the very large Queen Salote of Tonga was accompanied by the very small Sultan of Kelantan. When Noël Coward was asked who the latter was, he quipped, 'Her lunch'.

4 The first coronation to be televised was that of George VI. The reception was not very good and only a few people had sets. But it was a beginning.

5 The State coach is used by the Sovereign for the journey to the Abbey. It was commissioned for George III, though it was not ready in time for him to use it. Instead, he and his wife were carried in sedan chairs. One of its problems was its bad suspension. The 'Sailor King', William IV, compared its motion to that of a ship in a rough sea. It was not until the coronation of Elizabeth II that they got it right.

6 Edward VII's coronation had to be postponed by illness: the King had to have his appendix removed.

7 George VI described the discomforts of the journey to the Abbey. The suspension of the State coach had not yet been improved.

8 Wine, so to speak, was on the house at the coronations of Henry VIII and his daughter, Queen Mary.

9 Special tube trains were run from Kensington High Street to Westminster for peers and MPs attending the coronations of George VI and Elizabeth II.

10 The Earl Marshal is responsible for organizing the coronation (also for state funerals, but not Royal funerals). This is an hereditary appointment that has belonged to the Dukes of Norfolk since 1672.

11 King George IV refused to allow his wife, Queen Caroline, to attend his coronation. She was not entirely sane, and he was afraid she might embarrass him.

12 A number of Labour peers refused to attend the coronation of King George VI. The reason was not so much that they could not afford the robes (about £150 each), but a gesture. Labour MP James Maxton, for example, wished to see Buckingham Palace, Windsor Castle, and Holyrood turned into 'social institutions for the benefit of the people of this country'.

13 The coronation ceremony used to be held in the great hall of the Palace of Westminster, interrupted by a short service of consecration at the neighbouring Abbey. Afterwards, an enormous banquet was held. During that of William IV, local residents complained at the noise. When his successor, Queen Victoria, was crowned, the entire ceremony took place in the Abbey.

14 During the ceremony in the Palace of Westminster, the King's Champion used to ride in, throw down his gauntlet, and thrice challenge anyone to dispute the new Monarch's claim to the throne. Since the coronation of George IV in 1821, the Champion (which is another hereditary appointment) has had the less spectacular task of carrying the standard of England at the religious ceremony.

15 The shire horses are provided by Whitbread to haul the Speaker's coach.

Royalty and marriage

1 What Royal's father-in-law used to be concerned with the manufacture of pies and sausages?

2 Which Royal's wife had an ancestor who may have saved the life of George Washington during the American War of Independence?

3 Who proposed to his future wife without having met her?

4 Who was the first Royal to be married in St Paul's Cathedral?

5 The first Queen married him; the second Queen fought him. Who was he?

6 Where did the wedding of Queen Victoria and Prince Albert take place?

7 Who described his wife as 'the most perfect companion a man could wish for'?

8 Who was the best man to Prince Philip at his wedding?

9 Whose wife was notorious for her unpunctuality?

10 Who wished her wedding to be as simple as possible?

11 What is the Royal Marriage Act?

12 Which Royal had to renounce his right to succession before getting married?

13 Who was the Royal that danced a jig in his underwear at his brother's marriage?

14 Which Royal was given a complete cinema as a wedding present – and who gave it?

15 Which Royal, apart from the present Prince of Wales, proposed to a Lady Diana Spencer?

Answers   Royalty and marriage

1　The father of Captain Mark Phillips, husband of Princess Anne, used to be a director of Walls – makers of pies and sausages as well as icecream.

2　The Duchess of Windsor had an ancestor who is reputed to have put himself between George Washington and the sharp end of a British soldier's sabre.

3　George IV, when Prince of Wales, married Caroline of Brunswick in an attempt to write off his debts. When he first set eyes on his fiancée, he cried, 'I am not well, pray get me a glass of brandy'.

4　The Prince of Wales and Lady Diana Spencer were the first Royal couple to be married in St Paul's.

5　Queen Mary I married King Philip of Spain. After her death, Philip tried to marry Queen Elizabeth I. She declined and one of the results was the defeat of the Spanish Armada.

6　Queen Victoria and Prince Albert were married quietly in the Chapel Royal at St James's Palace.

7　Prince Albert used these adulatory remarks when writing to his brother about Queen Victoria.

8　Prince Philip's best man was his cousin David, Marquess of Milford Haven. Although he was referred to as 'Prince' Philip, he had yet to become a Prince officially. He was married as Lieutenant Philip Mount-batten RN.

9　Queen Alexandra, wife of Edward VII, was seldom punctual. When Alexandra was Princess of Wales, Queen Victoria wrote that, 'She is never ready for breakfast, not being out of her room till 11 ; and often Bertie [as he was known: his first name was Albert] breakfasts alone, and then she alone.'

10　Princess Anne wished her wedding to be as quiet as possible. Admittedly only one head of state – Prince Rainier – was invited, but 50 TV cameras were also present.

11　The gist of the Royal Marriage Act is it is illegal for any descendant of George II (it was George III who was instrumental in bringing it about) to marry without the consent of the reigning Sovereign. The penalties (in theory, at any rate) include loss of civil rights and, even, imprisonment. There are ways of getting round it, but they have never been used.

12　Prince Michael of Kent had to renounce his right of succession when he married Baroness Marie-Christine von Reibnitz. The Princess is a Roman Catholic.

13　King Henry VIII, then a dashing and jovial Prince, danced a jig at the wedding of his brother, Prince Arthur, to Catherine of Aragon.

14　Princess Elizabeth (now Queen Elizabeth II) and Prince Philip received a set of cinematograph equipment from Earl Mountbatten and his wife.

15　Frederick, Prince of Wales – son of George II – proposed to a Lady Diana Spencer. His father prohibited the match, and he married Augusta of Saxe-Gotha instead. They had nine children.

Royalty as trend-setters

1   Which Royal affected the way in which men knotted their ties – and, indeed, had a knot named after him?

2   Which Royal, by example, encouraged young women to throw away their high-heeled shoes – and to invest in flat heels?

3   Which Royal caused men to change their ideas on the way in which trousers should be pressed?

4   Which Royal made a type of hat named a 'toque' famous – if not generally popular?

5   Which Royals helped to lift sales of a new kind of car from the doldrums to the heights of success?

6   Which Royal did a great deal to encourage scientific research?

7   Which Royal began a craze for sea bathing – which has long endured?

8   Which Royal helped to make whisky popular?

9   Which Royal caused many young women to change their hair styles from the drab to the elegant?

10 Which Royal has some small influence upon the way in which people decorate their homes?

Answers   Royalty as trend-setters

1   The Duke of Windsor, when Prince of Wales, formed a habit of tying his ties with unusually large knots – a taste that persisted for the rest of his life. Anyone who cared to follow his example could use the 'full Windsor' or (if they preferred something slightly smaller) the 'half-Windsor'. He once denied responsibility for starting this vogue, but he none the less received credit for it.

2   The Princess of Wales prefers flat-heeled shoes for the sensible reason that they diminish her height. (They must also be more comfortable, when she has to stand for a long time at public engagements.)

3   King Edward VII's valet once, when his mind was presumably on something else, pressed his master's trousers fore and aft – instead of, as was the custom, putting the creases at the sides. The King liked it, and creases promptly changed direction.

4   Queen Mary, wife of George V was nearly always to be seen wearing a toque. One of its features was that it had no brim, and thus gave people a better view of her face.

5   Princess Margaret and the Earl of Snowdon bought a Mini for their journeys in London. After that, sales of this revolutionary little car – which had been hanging fire – took off.

6   Charles II, despite his reputation for being a fun-loving Monarch, did much to encourage science – not least by founding the Royal Society. He also encouraged the theatre: though, after the drabness of life during the Commonwealth, this needed little effort.

7   George III was persuaded that sea bathing was good for the health. He used to travel to Weymouth in Dorset, where he stayed at what is now the Gloucester Hotel. As HM emerged into the water from the bathing machine, an attendant band dutifully struck up the national anthem. Later, his son, the Prince Regent, took a similar view – though he preferred Brighton. Thus the resort became popular, and attracted the ailing or effete who, previously, had used the spa at Tunbridge Wells in Kent.

8   Queen Victoria did much to make whisky popular in England (in Scotland, people needed no such example). She used to enjoy a tot or two before retiring – especially when she was staying at Balmoral. The Queen and Prince Albert also made tartan respectable. After the rebellion of the '45, it had been rigorously suppressed.

9   The elegant Princess of Wales caused many women to look critically at their hair-do's and then to imitate her. It could be said that Princess Di (if she will excuse the familiarity) is a trend in herself.

10   Princess Michael of Kent is an interior decorator and has her own business.

Who said ?

1 'Bugger Bognor'.

2 'Put those damned clocks right'.

3 'This is a pretty kettle-of-fish'.

4 'I do not like bishops'. And (on being reminded that there was one of whom this particular Royal did approve) insisted, 'Ah – I like the man, but not the bishop'.

5 'There are not many candlelit moments to destroy'.

6 'It is worth being shot at – to see how much one is loved'.

7 'Were it not for my ability to see the funny side of my life, I would have been committed to an institution long ago'.

8 '(He is) the greatest beast in the world, and I heartily wish he were out of it'.

9 'We know from experience what it means to be away from those we love most of all'.

10 'If this goes on, I shall give up. I shall abdicate'.

11 'I am on a dreary sad pinnacle of solitary grandeur'.

12 Who, on being asked what she does when her husband wants something which she disapproves of, is reputed to have said, 'Oh I just tell him he shall have it and make sure he doesn't get it'?

13 'I hate all Boets and Bainters'.

14 'Let the boy win his spurs'.

15 'He speaks to me as if I was a public meeting'.

Answers   Who said?

1   King George V is said to have uttered these words when, at the end of his final illness, he was assured that he would soon be taken to Bognor to recuperate. However, *The Times* may have been more accurate, when it reported his last words as 'How is the Empire?'

2   Edward VIII is reputed to have said this shortly after the death of his father at Sandringham in 1936. It was George V's custom to insist that all the clocks should be kept half-an-hour fast.

3   Queen Mary is reputed to have said 'This is a pretty kettle-of-fish' when hearing of her son's infatuation for Mrs Wallis Simpson, later the Duchess of Windsor.

4   Queen Victoria expressed a dislike of bishops when the Houses of Convocation (Canterbury and York) held a reception to celebrate her Diamond Jubilee. The bishops were all attired in black, and their clothes looked shoddy.

5   Prince Andrew protested, in an interview with David Frost, that there had not been 'many candlelit moments'. He was speaking of the attention of the press and its effect on the more romantic side of his life.

6   Queen Victoria said that it was worth being shot at – after a mentally retarded youth named Roderick McLean had fired at her carriage outside Windsor station.

7   Prince Charles remarked upon the necessity of a sense of humour in his job.

8   King George II's wife, Caroline, uttered these harsh words about her son Frederick Prince of Wales. It could be argued that her wish was granted. After producing nine children, the Prince died of a fit of coughing and never came to the throne.

9   Queen Elizabeth II (as Princess Elizabeth) spoke of the pangs of separation on BBC's 'Children's Hour' in 1940. She was offering words of encouragement to children who were to be evacuated to America and thus removed from their parents.

10   King Edward VII threatened to abdicate (but probably did not mean it), when suffering from the illness (appendicitis) that caused his coronation to be postponed.

11   Queen Victoria was on 'this dreary sad pinnacle' after the death of her husband, Prince Albert.

12   The Queen.

13   George I was speaking of his dislike for those engaged in the arts, when he expressed hatred of 'Boets and Bainters'. The 'Bs' were not the result of a cold in the head. His Majesty had a very imperfect command of English.

14   Edward III insisted that his son, the Black Prince, should be allowed to win his spurs at Crécy – when one of his advisers suggested that the lad should be withdrawn to some less dangerous part of the battlefield.

15   Queen Victoria was speaking of the way in which Mr Gladstone addressed her.

Royalty and death

1 Which King apologized for taking such a long time to die?

2 What is the difference between a Royal Funeral and a State Funeral?

3 At whose funeral did the misbehaviour of a horse create a new custom?

4 Which Royal died of typhoid fever – despite his efforts to create more sanitary homes for the working classes?

5 Which Royal came to abhor the use of black at funerals?

6 Which Royal, on being told that – as an act of respect for his late father – St George's Chapel, Windsor, would be draped in black for his marriage, threatened to bring his wife to the ceremony in a hearse?

7 Which Royal death was mourned at the Trooping of the Colour by pipers of the Scots Guards playing 'The Flowers of the Forest'?

8 After whose death did somebody say 'Then I shall see another star in the sky'?

9 Which Royal supervised the design of a VIP's funeral car?

10 Whose funeral was attended by nine Kings?

Answers   Royalty and death

1   According to Macaulay, Charles II '... had been, he said, an unconscionable time dying; but he hoped that they would excuse it'.

2   A State Funeral (organized by the Earl Marshal) is paid for by the state. A Royal Funeral (organized by the Lord Chamberlain) is not. Only the Sovereign is accorded the former automatically, and there have been very few exceptions. Nelson, the Duke of Wellington, and Sir Winston Churchill received State Funerals. In each case, the reigning Monarch gave the necessary assent.

3   When the gun-carriage was waiting outside the station at Windsor, ready to convey the body of Queen Victoria to St George's Chapel, one of the horses snapped its traces. At the suggestion of an ADC, the beasts were replaced by members of the Naval guard of honour. Ever since, the gun-carriage (provided by the Royal Horse Artillery) has been hauled by 138 Naval ratings.

4   Prince Albert died of typhoid fever at Windsor Castle. Although an exhibit at the Great Exhibition of 1851 (which was his responsibility) featured model homes for the workers, the sanitary conditions at Windsor Castle were far from adequate.

5   Having studied accounts of funerals carried out at St Peter's in Rome, Queen Victoria was impressed by the use of colour. It was, she felt, suitable for a thanksgiving, which was what a funeral should be – a

thanksgiving for the life that had ended. For her own funeral, Victoria insisted that the streets of London should be adorned with purple cashmere decorated with white satin bows.

6   Before Queen Victoria acquired her aversion to black, she proposed to use black drapes at St George's Chapel (as yet another act of mourning for her beloved Albert) when her son, the Prince of Wales, was married there. The Prince's retort was effective. Black was not used.

7   When he died, the Duke of Windsor, after so many years in self-imposed exile, was brought back to Windsor for interment at Frogmore. The funeral took place on the day following the Trooping of the Colour – at which the Queen ordered 'The Flowers of the Forest' to be played as an act of remembrance.

8   The words are attributed to a Zulu chief on hearing of the death of 'the great White Queen' – i.e. Queen Victoria.

9   Prince Albert designed the Duke of Wellington's funeral car. In the matter of the coffin, the Prince's enthusiasm seems to have run away with him. It was uncommonly large, whilst the Duke was quite a small man.

10   Nine Monarchs, including the Kaiser, attended the funeral of Edward VII. It was the last occasion in which it was possible to assemble so many European crowned heads in one place.

Royalty and regalia

1 Which King's crown was found beneath a hedge after a battle?

2 Who stole the Crown Jewels from the Tower of London – and nearly got away with it?

3 Who ordered the Crown Jewels to be melted down and sold?

4 Which crown contains the famous Koh-i-noor diamond, once insured for £2 million?

5 Who owns the Crown Jewels?

6 Who provided the Queen (then Princess Elizabeth) with the tiara she wore at her wedding?

7 What was the design of the coronation ring worn by Queen Elizabeth II?

8 At the coronation ceremony, one crown is exchanged for another. What are the two crowns?

9 Who admitted that, during the coronation ceremony, 'Yes, the crown does get rather heavy'?

10 What is the largest gem in the sceptre?

11 When Charles II came to the throne, there was no regalia for his coronation. How much did the set of replacements cost?

12 At what battle did a King wear a stone known as the Black Prince's Ruby in his helmet?

13 At whose coronation did the Archbishop of Canterbury try to force the ring on to the wrong finger?

14 What crown may (though it is not certain) contain the ear-rings of Queen Elizabeth I?

15 What crown does the Queen wear for the annual State Opening of Parliament?

1   The crown of Richard III was found beneath a hedge after he had been killed at the Battle of Bosworth in 1485.

2   Colonel Blood, an Irish adventurer, led an attempt to steal the Crown Jewels in 1671. Blood was captured while trying to escape, and the stolen regalia was recovered. King Charles was amused at his audacity: far from punishing him, he restored Blood's Irish estates to him and gave him a pension of £500 a year.

3   Cromwell melted the gold of the regalia and sold it, along with the jewels, after the Civil War. The whole collection fetched a mere £2,647.

4   The Koh-i-noor diamond is reputed to bring good luck to any woman who wears it; but bad luck to a man. It was incorporated in a crown manufactured in 1937 for the Queen Consort – now the Queen Mother.

5   The Crown Jewels are the property of the state – not of the Sovereign.

6   Her grandmother, Queen Mary, gave Princess Elizabeth a tiara as a wedding present – though the one that she wore at the ceremony belonged to her mother.

7   The coronation ring contained a large sapphire set with four rubies in the shape of a cross.

8   At the coronation, the Crown of St Edward is exchanged for the Imperial State Crown. The former has little to do with St Edward: it was manufactured for Charles II. The latter was made for the coronation of Queen Victoria. There were fears that the Crown of St Edward might be too big for her.

9   Queen Elizabeth II remarked on the heaviness of the crown – though she did not specify which.

10   The largest gem in the Sceptre of the Cross (in fact, there are two sceptres – the other is known as the Rod with the Dove) is a diamond named the Great Star of Africa.

11   The cost of producing a complete set of regalia for the coronation of Charles II was £31,978.

12   The Black Prince's Ruby was worn in the helmet of Henry V at Agincourt. Now it is in the Imperial Crown.

13   Queen Victoria's coronation. The Archbishop attempted to force the ring on to the wrong finger – and thus caused the Sovereign considerable pain.

14   The ear-rings of Queen Elizabeth I may be in the Imperial Crown. Four drop pearls are credited with this distinction.

15   The Queen wears the Imperial Crown at the State Opening of Parliament.

Royal Yachts

1   Which Royal Yacht was moored permanently in the Thames off Whitehall?

2   Which Royal Yacht, on completion, turned out to be unstable and had to be substantially modified?

3   Whose yacht, on the death of her owner, was sunk off the Isle of Wight?

4   In which Royal Yacht was/is displayed, the flag flown from Captain R.F. Scott's sledge on his journey to the South Pole?

5   What was the largest number of steam yachts that Queen Victoria owned all at one time?

6   From what Royal Yacht was a sea monster observed?

7   What liner did duty as a Royal Yacht during the present Monarch's reign?

8   What is the rank of the commanding officer of the present Royal Yacht?

9   How many flags are unfurled when the *Britannia* dresses ship?

10 What is remarkable about *Britannia*'s main mast?

11 What Royal Yacht had/has a table designed by Prince Albert in the ante-room of the state apartments?

12 What was the name of the first Royal Steam Yacht?

13 The 50-foot long boom of an erstwhile Royal Sailing Yacht now does duty as a flagstaff. Where?

14 What is peculiar about the dress of the Royal Yacht's naval ratings?

15 What Royal Yacht ran into another ship, killing the latter's master and two passengers?

Answers Royal Yachts

1 Charles II escaped to France from a creek near Brighton in a 34-ton coal brig named *Surprise*. After the Restoration, the King acquired her, renamed her *Royal Escape*, and ordered that she should take up permanent moorings in the Thames.

2 The last yacht to be named *Victoria and Albert* was completed at the beginning of this century. Initially, she was top heavy: the funnels had to be shortened, the forecastle removed, a lot of ballast added, and several particularly heavy fittings removed. The bill came to £½ million – almost as much as she had cost in the first place.

3 King George V's racing yacht *Britannia* was sunk off St Catherine's Point on the Isle of Wight after he had died in 1936. The sinking was carried out in accordance with the late Monarch's instructions.

4 Captain Scott's flag is to be seen in the present Royal Yacht, *Britannia*.

5 At one time, Queen Victoria owned no fewer than seven steam yachts – though she was not particularly fond of the sea.

6 A sea monster was observed from the bridge of the Prince of Wales's (later Edward VII) steam yacht *Osborne*. The ship was on passage off the north coast of Sicily at the time. Her owner was not on deck.

7 The Shaw Savill & Albion liner *Gothic* served as Royal Yacht during much of the Queen's Commonwealth tour of 1953-54. *Britannia* was not ready for service until the end of the tour – when she brought the Queen home from Malta.

8 The Royal Yacht is commanded by a Rear-Admiral, who is known as The Flag Officer Royal Yachts. He is a member of the Royal Household.

9 Forty-eight flags and pennants are unfurled when *Britannia* dresses ship. This well-drilled operation takes only three seconds.

10 The mainmast of *Britannia* has a hinge in it, so that the top twenty feet can be lowered to enable her to pass underneath the bridges over the Saint Lawrence Seaway.

11 The *Britannia* has a table in her ante-room that was designed by Prince Albert. Using gimbals, the Prince had hoped to keep the top steady in bad weather.

12 The first Royal Steam Yacht was completed in 1843, after Queen Victoria had complained about the time it took to travel to Scotland in a sailing ship. She was named *Victoria and Albert*. All told, three Royal Yachts bore that name.

13 The 50-ft boom of George V's sailing yacht *Britannia* now serves as a flagstaff in the grounds of Carisbrooke Castle on the Isle of Wight.

14 The Royal Yachtsmen (as they are called) wear little black bows on the waistbands of their trousers to perpetuate the mourning for Prince Albert.

15 One of Queen Victoria's steam yachts, the *Alberta,* collided with a schooner named *Mistletoe,* killing the latter's captain and two of his passengers.

Royal idiosyncrasies

1   Which King, on coming to the throne, could not speak a word of English?

2   Which Sovereign insisted that smokers staying at Windsor should not light up until he/she had retired for the night? (It may be a clue, but it is only fair to say that this was before smoking had become medically accepted as a health hazard.)

3   Which King, in a moment of pique, hurled the Garter Emblem through a porthole of the Royal Yacht?

4   Which Royal refused to eat on a train when travelling in the UK, but was prepared to do so on the Continent?

5   Which Royal was handicapped by a stammer?

6   Which Royal gave away his sporting guns upon the insistence of his wife?

7   Which Royal would only agree to the installation of electric light in the Royal Yacht after a long argument with an occulist – and never accepted it in a Royal train?

8   Which Royal compelled his weekend guests to devote much of their time to gardening?

9   Which Royal had a passion for speed, and was always urging the chauffeur to overtake the car in front?

10 Which Royal regarded ivy as a nasty weed and spent much time removing it from the garden of her host?

11 Which King is said to have cried when he learnt that he had to take over the throne?

12 Which Royal encouraged a friend in his attempt to become a pop singer?

1   George I, who was the Elector of Hanover, could speak only German when he became King of Great Britain.

2   Queen Victoria.

3   King Edward VII objected to the suggestion that the Order of the Garter should be conferred upon the Shah of Persia. When a specially designed non-Christian version of the Garter star and badge was submitted to him aboard the *Victoria and Albert*, he flung it through a porthole. It was caught by a sailor in a steam pinnace outside.

4   Queen Victoria would never eat in the Royal train. On the other hand, she had a healthy appetite when travelling to the South of France on holiday.

5   King George VI was handicapped by a stammer.

6   Prince Charles gave his sporting guns to Prince Andrew. The Princess of Wales is greatly opposed to blood sports.

7   Queen Victoria had a considerable mistrust of electricity.

8   Edward VIII (both as King and Prince of Wales) had a country retreat at Fort Belvedere near Virginia Water. The grounds were overgrown, and the Prince (or King) enlisted the help of his male guests in his efforts to clear away the weeds.

9   Edward VII, whether travelling by car or train, liked things to move quickly.

10   During the Second World War, Queen Mary spent nearly all her time at the Duke of Beaufort's estate at Badminton. Her Majesty industriously employed herself trying to eradicate the ivy in the grounds.

11   King George VI, the man who never wanted to be King, was greatly upset when he learned of the intended abdication of his brother, Edward VIII, and that he would have to assume the throne.

12   Princess Margaret encouraged the efforts of her friend, Roddy Llewellyn, to become a pop star. The enterprise was not entirely successful.

Royal bodyguards

1   Who provides the Sovereign's Escort for ceremonial occasions?

2   For the membership of which Royal bodyguard is a sufficient skill at archery an essential qualification?

3   Which Royal bodyguard was mobilized to defend St James's Palace against violence during the Chartist Riots of 1848?

4   Which Royal bodyguard used to insist that its members had beards – a custom that survived until 1936?

5   Which is the oldest of the Royal bodyguards?

6   Which Royal bodyguard was unable to catch up with the Sovereign because the Royal Yacht was twenty-four hours late in arriving?

7   Which Royal bodyguard attended King Henry VIII at the Field of the Cloth of Gold?

8   The posts of (a) Captain of The Yeoman of the Guard and (b) The Honourable Corps of Gentlemen at Arms are both by tradition given to people eminent in another sphere. Who are they?

9   Royal bodyguards are for ceremonial – part of the Royal tradition. In practice, upon whom does the safety of the Queen depend at such London events as Trooping the Colour?

10   One of the Royal bodyguards was mounted and, when its uniform was redesigned in 1840, the new outfit was modelled on that of an officer in the dragoons. Which bodyguard?

11   What is the difference between the Yeomen of the Guard in real life and the Yeomen of the Guard in the Gilbert and Sullivan opera?

12   Which Royal bodyguard was founded at the behest of Queen Anne in 1704?

Answers Royal bodyguards

1 The Household Cavalry – i.e. The Life Guards and The Blues and Royals (formerly The Royal Horse Guards and the 1st Dragoon Guards). Both The Life Guards and The Royal Horse Guards were formed immediately after the Civil War.

2 The Royal Company of Archers – or, as George IV called them, the Royal Bodyguard for Scotland.

3 The Honourable Corps of Gentlemen at Arms. In fact, the Chartists did not attack the palace and no shots were fired.

4 The Yeomen of the Guard were required to have Tudor-style beards until 1936, when Edward VIII decided that it was no longer necessary.

5 The Yeomen of the Guard is the oldest. It was founded by Henry VII.

6 The Royal Company of Archers was thrown into confusion when the Royal Yacht was twenty-four hours late in arriving at Leith in 1842. A squadron of dragoons was used instead. The Archers eventually assembled, but they could not keep up with the trotting cavalrymen. Wrote the Queen, 'The Body Guard were . . . dreadfully pushed about'.

7 The Honourable Corps of Gentlemen at Arms – which was, indeed, Henry VIII's creation.

8 The Captain of the Yeomen of the Guard is, by tradition, the Government Deputy Chief Whip in the House of Lords; and, of the Honourable Corps of Gentlemen at Arms, the Government Chief Whip in the House of Lords.

9 'A' Division of the Metropolitan Police, which has its headquarters at Cannon Row off Whitehall, is responsible for the overall security pattern. Members of the Royal protection branch have undergone special training, wear plain clothes, and are armed. Outside the capital, the police are reinforced by members of the local Special Branch departments.

10 The Honourable Corps of Gentlemen at Arms used to be mounted.

11 The Yeomen of the Guard in the Gilbert and Sullivan opera were really The Yeomen Warders of the Tower of London. They are employees of the Department of the Environment.

12 Queen Anne was responsible for founding the Royal Company of Archers.

The Royal Household

1   Which member of the Royal Household writes thrillers under the pen-name of 'Michael Sinclair'?

2   Which member of the Royal Household has a white staff of office, which he snaps in two, and drops into the grave of a dead Sovereign?

3   Who is the Clerk of the Closet?

4   Who looks after the Royal accounts?

5   Which of a Sovereign's equerries fell in love with a Princess?

6   Who supervises the Queen's ladies-in-waiting?

7   Three members of the Royal Household are appointed by Parliament. Which?

8   Which member of the Royal Household remains at Buckingham Palace when the Queen opens Parliament – as hostage for her safe return?

9   Who is head of the Royal Household?

10   Who was the first Poet Laureate?

11   Who became Queen Victoria's private secretary?

12   Who is responsible for the domestic organization of Buckingham Palace?

13   Which private secretary to a Sovereign received a knighthood in a Royal train?

14   Which former Comptroller of the Household was killed by an IRA bomb?

15   Who is head of the Household in Scotland?

Answers The Royal Household

1   Michael Shea – Press Secretary to the Queen.

2   The Lord Chamberlain. It signifies the end of his service to the late Monarch, and the successor's freedom to appoint a new household.

3   The Clerk of the Closet is a post occupied by the Bishop of Bath and Wells. Its original task was to resolve the Sovereign's doubts 'about spiritual matters'.

4   The Keeper of the Privy Purse is in charge of the Royal accounts – including those of the Duchy of Lancaster. He also attends to the financial administration of Sandringham and Balmoral (the Queen's private estates) and the Royal stud.

5   Group Captain Peter Townsend, equerry to George VI, fell in love with Princess Margaret.

6   The Mistress of the Robes (who, in fact, now has nothing to do with the robes) supervises the ladies-in-waiting – who, to be more precise, are variously known as 'Ladies of the Bedchamber' and 'Women of the Bedchamber'.

7   The Treasurer to the Queen, the Comptroller, and the Vice Chamberlain are all appointed by Parliament.

8   The Vice Chamberlain remains at the Palace during the state opening of Parliament.

9   The Lord Chamberlain is head of the household, though his duties are mostly concerned with ceremonial matters.

10   John Dryden, in 1668, was the first poet to be officially appointed to the post. He was also required to undertake the job of court historian.

11   Prince Albert.

12   The Master of the Household – assisted by the palace steward and the chief housekeeper.

13   King George VI conferred a knighthood on his private secretary, Alan Lascelles, when travelling from Niagara to Washington during the 1939 Royal tour of Canada and the USA.

14   Sir Anthony Berry was killed by an IRA bomb at the 1984 Conservative conference in Brighton.

15   The Hereditary Lord High Constable, the Earl of Erroll, is the senior member of the household in Scotland.

Royal addresses

1 What is the London home of the Queen Mother?

2 Who live at Kensington Palace?

3 Who bought Gatcombe Park in Gloucestershire, and who live in it?

4 Which Royal has a house on what Caribbean island?

5 Who lived at Park House, Sandringham?

6 Who was given a stately home in Kent?

7 The Prince of Wales's country home is named Highgrove House. What is the nearest town?

8 Whose London address is 22 Friary Court?

9 What future King was born and christened at White Lodge, Richmond Park?

10 What future Monarch was born at 17 Bruton Street, Mayfair – and, during childhood, lived at 145 Piccadilly?

Answers   **Royal addresses**

1   Clarence House.

2   The Prince and Princess of Wales and Princess Margaret.

3   The Queen bought Gatcombe Park, a 73-acre estate and mansion in Gloucestershire, as a country retreat for Princess Anne and Captain Mark Phillips. It is near the home of Captain Phillips's parents, and handy for horse trials at Badminton.

4   Princess Margaret owns a house on the island of Mustique. It is one of the Windward Islands.

5   The Princess of Wales.

6   Chevening in Kent, the ancestral home of the Earls of Stanhope, was presented to the Prince of Wales. He seldom used it.

7   The nearest town to Highgrove is Tetbury in Gloucestershire.

8   Princess Alexandra and her husband, the Hon. Angus Ogilvy. Friary Court is part of St James's Palace.

9   The future King Edward VIII (later the Duke of Windsor) was born at White Lodge, Richmond, in 1894.

10   Queen Elizabeth II. The Bruton Street address was the London home of her maternal grandfather, the Earl of Strathmore. The house in Piccadilly belonged to the Queen's father when he was Duke of York.

Other titles

The following are better known by some other name.

1 Who is the Duke of Lancaster?

2 Who is the Duke of Cornwall?

3 Who is Lord of the Isles and Great Steward of Scotland?

4 Who is Countess of Snowdon?

5 Who is Lord High Admiral of the United Kingdom?

6 Who is Earl of Merioneth and Baron Greenwich?

7 Who is Earl of Carrick and Baron Renfrew?

8 Who is Earl of Saint Andrews and Baron Downpatrick?

9 Who is Earl of Ulster and Baron Culloden?

10 Who is HRH Prince George?

11 Who is HRH Princess Alice?

12 Who was once the Duchess of York?

Answers Other titles

1   The Queen (it should be noted that she is *not* described as the Duchess of Lancaster).

2   The Prince of Wales.

3   The Prince of Wales.

4   Princess Margaret.

5   The Queen.

6   Prince Philip, Duke of Edinburgh.

7   The Prince of Wales.

8   The Duke of Kent.

9   The Duke of Gloucester.

10 The Duke of Kent.

11 Princess Alice is the widow of the present Duke of Gloucester's father.

12 The Queen Mother.

Which regiment?

A member of the Royal Family is Colonel-in-Chief of each of the following regiments. Which Royal; which regiment?

1 The Royal Tank Regiment.

2 The 14th/20 King's Hussars.

3 The 15th/19 King's Royal Hussars.

4 The Parachute Regiment.

5 The Gordon Highlanders.

6 The Royal Green Jackets.

7 The Queen's Own Highlanders.

8 2nd Edward VII's Own Gurkha Rifles.

9 The Royal Highland Fusiliers.

10 The 17th/21 Lancers.

11 The Royal Regiment of Fusiliers.

12 The Honourable Artillery Company.

13 The Royal Regiment of Wales.

14 The Worcestershire and Sherwood Foresters Regiment.

15 The 9th/12 Royal Lancers.

Answers   Which regiment?

1 The Queen.
2 Princess Anne.
3 Princess Margaret.
4 The Prince of Wales.
5 The Prince of Wales.
6 The Queen.
7 Prince Philip.
8 The Prince of Wales.
9 Princess Margaret.
10 Princess Alexandra.
11 The Duke of Kent.
12 The Queen.
13 The Prince of Wales.
14 Princess Anne.
15 The Queen Mother.

Royal babies

1 Which Royal was born in Norfolk on a July day in 1961, and weighed 7 lb 12 oz at birth?

2 Who, just after he was born, was described by his father as 'a sweet little boy' – and, in later years, remarked: 'I imagine this was the last time my father was ever inspired to apply this precise appellation'?

3 Who was born at Glamis Castle in Scotland and weighed in at 6 lb 11 oz?

4 Which two Princesses were both delivered by Caesarean section?

5 Where was the birth of Prince Harry registered?

6 Which two future Kings were given Albert as their first names when they were christened – and yet used another name when they came to the throne?

7 The attendance of the Home Secretary used to be required at a Royal birth. Who was the first child of a Sovereign to be born without the need for his presence?

8 Who was playing squash with his private secretary when his first child was born?

9 Which Royal was expected in October, but arrived in November?

10 Who was born at a hospital in Paddington, and clocked up 7 lb $1\frac{1}{2}$ oz when first put on the scales?

11 What Royal, when asked if he wanted a large family, exclaimed, 'Bloody hell – give us a chance!'?

12 Which Royal mother made a long journey across Germany, crossed the Channel, and arrived at Kensington Palace just in time for the birth of her daughter?

Answers   Royal babies

1   The Princess of Wales.

2   The Duke of Windsor.

3   Princess Margaret.

4   Princess Elizabeth (later Queen Elizabeth II) and Princess Margaret.

5   The Westminster Registrar went to Kensington Palace to register Prince Harry's birth. His father, Prince Charles, gave his occupation as 'Prince of the United Kingdom'. The baby Prince was also given his National Health Insurance number – LSCVT275.

6   Edward VII and George VI. Queen Victoria had insisted that no King should be named Albert. This was out of respect for her late husband – who, at one time, she would have liked to have been called King Albert.

7   Prince Charles was the first baby to be born without this rather senseless piece of tradition.

8   Prince Philip was playing squash when Prince Charles was born. Times changed. Prince Charles was present when both his babies were born.

9   Again: Prince Charles.

10   Prince William (and Prince Harry, too) was born in the Lindo Wing of St Mary's Hospital, Paddington. Prince William weighed 7 lb $1\frac{1}{2}$ oz.

11   Prince Charles – after the birth of Prince William.

12   The Duchess of Kent, mother of Queen Victoria. A fortune teller had once told the Duke that he would become the father of a great Queen. He believed her: hence the need for his child to be born in England. The journey from Germany was made rather late in the day – due to problems over the Duke of Kent's finances.

Royal hobbies

1 Which Royal was an enthusiastic stamp collector? And in what stamps was he particularly interested?

2 Which Royal enjoys working on intricate jigsaw puzzles?

3 Which Royal can play the cello?

4 Which Royal liked to do needlework – once described it as 'my secret vice'?

5 Which Royal had a famous dolls' house?

6 Which Royal had a passion for collecting things – anything, indeed, from firearms to theatrical prints?

7 Which Royal was never happier than when playing cards?

8 Which Royal had above-average talents as a water-colourist?

9 Which Royal is a motor racing enthusiast?

10 Which Royal won acclaim for his photographs of wildlife?

11 Which Royal won modest fame as a composer?

12 Which Royal liked to explore antiquarian bookshops, looking for second-hand volumes?

Answers   Royal hobbies

1 King George V. He started this hobby at the age of 25, when serving in the Royal Navy, and his collection was considerably enlarged in 1893, when fellow philatelists gave him 1,500 stamps as a wedding present. Not surprisingly, he was particularly interested in British and British Empire stamps. At the time of his death in 1936, he had filled 325 albums.

2 The Queen enjoys difficult jigsaw puzzles.

3 Prince Charles is a cellist.

4 Edward VIII was proficient at needlework. His mother, Queen Mary, taught him the art.

5 Queen Mary owned a famous dolls' house. Some of the books in its library were handwritten by famous contemporary authors.

6 George IV was an obsessive collector. (Queen Mary, wife of George V, was another, but the former's interests were wider. Among his theatrical items, were no fewer than 116 prints of the actor David Garrick.)

7 Edward VII had a passion for gambling and, in particular, for playing cards.

8 Queen Victoria could produce very attractive water-colours.

9 Prince Michael of Kent. He has also competed in several motor rallies.

10 Prince Philip. A selection of his work was published in *Birds from Britannia* – most of the shots were taken from the Royal Yacht.

11 Henry VIII was a talented composer. He had an impressive collection of musical instruments, which included twenty-six lutes.

12 Prince Albert was happier roaming around second-hand bookshops than indulging in the high life of court.

Royalty and horses

1 Which King's horse, when competing in the Derby, inadvertently caused the death of a woman?

2 For what was Burmese famous?

3 Where and when were the Royal studs founded?

4 Where were the majority of Prince Philip's polo ponies bred?

5 Which was the only horse to win the Derby with its jockey wearing the colours of a reigning Monarch?

6 Which Royal learned to ride on a pony named Greensleeves?

7 Who, riding Doublet, became European Champion and Sports Personality of 1971?

8 For what sport was Doublet originally intended?

9 Who presented George VI with five of the Windsor Greys used to haul the state coach at his daughter's coronation?

10 What was the name of the horse that Prince Charles rode in his first team cross-country event?

11 Which member of the Royal Family competed at the Munich Olympics of 1972?

12 Which Royal broke his collar-bone in a point-to-point?

13 Who gave up playing polo and took up carriage driving at the age of 50?

14 What famous foreign visitor rode a horse named Centennial, when accompanying the Queen on a ride in Windsor Home Park in 1982?

15 On what horse did the present Queen, then heir to the throne, first accompany her father to Trooping the Colour?

Answers Royalty and horses

1 At the Derby of 1913, a suffragette named Emily Davison burst out from the crowd and grabbed the bridle of King George V's horse, Anmer. Anmer fell : the jockey was thrown clear, but Miss Davison was crushed beneath and killed.

2 Burmese displayed amazing cool when ridden by the Queen to Trooping the Colour in 1981. A 17-year-old youth discharged six blank cartridges at Her Majesty. Burmese, admittedly, shied ; but the Queen brought him expertly under control.

3 The Royal studs were founded at Hampton Court in the sixteenth century.

4 The majority of Prince Philip's polo ponies were bred in Argentina.

5 Minoru, owned by Edward VII, won the Derby in 1909.

6 The Prince of Wales learned to ride on Greensleeves.

7 Princess Anne.

8 Doublet was reared as a polo pony.

9 The Queen of the Netherlands.

10 Mexico.

11 Captain Mark Phillips. He was not successful.

12 Edward VIII (when Prince of Wales). His father was displeased and cautioned him against competing in point-to-points.

13 The Duke of Edinburgh.

14 President Reagan. The Queen, incidentally, accompanied him on Burmese.

15 A hunter named Tommy.

Royalty and their pets

1 What Royal pet caused Buckingham Palace to be officially scheduled as a zoo?

2 What Royal pet took part in the procession at a state funeral?

3 Who owned a hamster named Chi-Chi, a rabbit named Harvey, and two South American lovebirds – the one named Davey Crockett and the other, Annie Oakley?

4 What dog accompanied his master into exile and later died of a bite from an adder?

5 What Royal owns a dachshund named Pipkin?

6 Who are Smoky, Shadow, Spark, Myth, Fable and Diamond?

7 What is a 'dorgi'?

8 Who was broken-hearted when a Siamese cat went missing and, later, was found to have been killed by a car?

9 Who breeds labradors?

10 Which Sovereign's first action after the coronation was to bath a dog?

Answers   Royalty and their pets

1   In 1930, Britain was alarmed by an outbreak of psittacosis – a disease not unlike influenza to which parrots and budgerigars are prone. As a result, imports of these birds were banned. At the time, George V was expecting the arrival from Brazil of a mate for his pet macaw. What, His Majesty wanted to know, could be done about it? After some thought, it was realized that the ban did not apply to zoological gardens under proper supervision. Thus Buckingham Palace was scheduled as a zoo – and the King got his macaw.

2   King Edward VII's fox-terrier Caesar was among the mourners in his funeral procession.

3   Prince Charles – when young.

4   A Cairn terrier named Slipper left England with the Duke of Windsor aboard the destroyer HMS *Fury*. Slipper was later sent to the future Duchess of Windsor at her temporary residence in France. It was during a walk with her that the little dog was killed by an adder.

5   Princess Margaret.

6   They are all corgis belonging to the Queen.

7   The Queen owns two 'dorgies' – Piper and Chipper. They are the products of an illicit love affair between one of the Corgis and Princess Margaret's dachshund.

8   Princess Michael of Kent. The London cat residents are a Siamese named Magi, and two Burmese – Jessie and Holly. At their Gloucestershire home, the Kents have a Persian (Spikey), a tabby (Triggy), and a black-and-white of no clearly defined ancestry that answers to Pussie.

9   The Queen – at Sandringham.

10   The first act of Queen Victoria after her coronation was to give her dog, Dash, a bath.

Who are (or were)?

1 Prinny?

2 Tum-tum?

3 May Blossom?

4 Uncle King?

5 Grandpapa England?

6 The Shop?

7 Brenda and Yvonne?

8 Batlugs?

9 Potty (or, sometimes, Glossipops)?

10 Our Val?

11 Brian?

12 What Royal godmother remarked, 'I suppose I'll now be known as "Charley's Aunt" '?

Answers   Who are (or were)?

1   George IV when Prince Regent.

2   Edward VII.

3   The young Victoria's maternal grandmother used to call her 'May Blossom'.

4   This was the young (and future) Queen Victoria's name for George IV.

5   This was Princess Elizabeth's (later Queen Elizabeth II) name for her grandfather, George V.

6   George VI used to call Buckingham Palace 'The Shop'.

7   The Queen and Princess Margaret as portrayed by *Private Eye*.

8   The future George VI was called 'Batlugs' by his fellow naval cadets – on account of his protruding ears.

9   Prince Henry, Duke of Gloucester – the father of the present Duke.

10   Princess Michael of Kent.

11   The Prince of Wales – again according to *Private Eye*.

12   Princess Margaret – on hearing that her nephew was to be christened Charles.

Ceremonial matters

1   What units in the British army fire Royal salutes in Hyde Park and at the Tower of London?

2   In which coach does the Queen travel to the State Opening of Parliament?

3   When was Trooping the Colour first carried out?

4   Who summons the House of Commons to the House of Lords on the occasion of the State Opening of Parliament?

5   Who is responsible for rehearsing a ceremonial procession?

6   For what two ceremonial occasions did the composer Handel contribute music?

7   What foreign Sovereign attended a state funeral wearing the uniform of a Field Marshal in the British army?

8   Who is the chief herald – and how many heralds are there?

9   When the footguard form up for changing the guard at Buckingham Palace, they usually assemble at Wellington Barracks. On certain days in May, however, they use the Horse Guards Parade Ground. When this happens, the officers are required to march in slow time across the parade ground to join their units. Who started this custom – and why?

10 At the Investiture of the Prince of Wales, the Prince replies to a loyal address made on behalf of the people of Wales. One Prince managed to deliver his speech in Welsh. Who?

11 What body of men still give three cheers for Charles II on their Founder's Day?

12 Who act as postillions and drive the horse-drawn coaches in ceremonial processions?

13 At what speed does a ceremonial procession travel?

14 What Sovereign refused to celebrate the silver jubilee of his/her reign?

15 What object to do with coronations was stolen on Christmas Day 1950 – and found in a Scottish abbey $3\frac{1}{2}$ months later?

Answers   Ceremonial matters

1   The King's Troop of the Royal Horse Artillery (it is always the *King's* Troop, even if the reigning Sovereign is a Queen) fires the salute in Hyde Park. The Honourable Artillery Company (a unit in the Territorial Army) fires the salute at the Tower.

2   The Queen travels from Buckingham Palace to Westminster in the Irish State Coach when she performs the opening of Parliament.

3   Trooping the Colour first celebrated the Sovereign's birthday in 1805. The soldiers on duty used to receive an extra day's pay.

4   The Gentleman Usher of the Black Rod. He carries out the task in his role of the Sovereign's Messenger.

5   The Crown Equerry – who is in charge of the Royal Mews at Buckingham Palace.

6   Handel's 'Water Music' was first played at a party held on the Thames by George I in 1717 – and, afterwards, accompanied the progress of the Sovereign in river pageants. For the coronation of George II in 1727, Handel set the anthem 'Zadok the priest . . . annointed Solomon King' to music.

7   The Kaiser attended King Edward VII's funeral dressed as a British Field Marshal. It was an honorary rank that had been bestowed upon him.

8   The chief herald is the Garter King of Arms. There are thirteen heralds in all.

9   The custom was instituted in the reign of George II. The object was to make sure that the officers were sober after their junketings on the previous evening.

10   Prince Charles.

11   The Chelsea pensioners. The Royal Hospital, Chelsea, was founded by Charles II as a home for veterans of his standing army.

12   The Queen's grooms from the Royal Mews.

13   Three miles an hour.

14   Queen Victoria refused to celebrate her Silver Jubilee because she was still mourning for Prince Albert – who had died in the previous year. However, she made up for it by having Golden and Diamond Jubilees to celebrate.

15   The Stone of Scone – which had lain beneath the Coronation Chair in Westminster Abbey ever since it had been removed from Scotland by Edward I in 1296 – was stolen on Christmas Day, 1950. On 11 April 1951, it was discovered on the high altar of the ruined abbey at Arbroath in Scotland.

Royal visits

1 Which Royal disembarked on to French soil from a bathing machine?

2 Which Royal used the exorbitant cost of being entertained as a punishment for incurring displeasure?

3 In what city did a dance floor collapse under the weight of numbers just before the arrival of a Royal guest?

4 Which Royal terrified his aides by proposing to travel in a wheelbarrow across a tightrope spanning the Niagara Falls?

5 According to a newspaper report, a certain Royal's 'unflappability was . . . severely tested' by the conduct of her host. Who was the Royal; and who the host?

6 Which Royals, on their return from a visit to foreign parts, brought with them the idea for a new type of warship that transformed the British fleet?

7 Which Royal received news of the Sovereign's death when staying at a hunting lodge in Kenya?

8 What was the last occasion on which Royalty set off in a battleship for a tour of distant lands?

9 On what Royal visit was an English King thrown by his host in a wrestling bout?

10 When did a British Sovereign fly faster than sound?

11 Where was the Sovereign greeted by a descendant of Fletcher Christian, leader of the *Bounty*'s mutineers?

12 To what prime minister did the Queen say, 'Thank you very much, Sir Walter Raleigh'?

Answers Royal visits

1 On a visit to Louis Philippe, then King of France, Queen Victoria was transported by bathing machine on the last part of her journey from the Royal Yacht to the shore.

2 Queen Elizabeth I. To take only one example, a visit to the Earl of Leicester at Kenilworth set her host back £1,000 a day.

3 The dance floor disaster occurred in New York, when Edward VII (as Prince of Wales) visited the city in 1860.

4 On the same visit to North America, Blondin offered to convey the Prince over Niagara Falls in a wheelbarrow. HRH was interested : the Duke of Newcastle had to dissuade him.

5 Ann Morrow of the *Daily Telegraph* was reporting the Queen's visit to Morocco, where King Hassan II was apt to keep his guests waiting, and to make sudden changes of plan.

6 Queen Victoria and Prince Albert were crossing Cherbourg harbour in the Royal Yacht's barge, when they noticed a new type of warship. Prince Albert pointed out its merits to the Admiralty, and work was begun on HMS *Warrior,* Britain's first battleship.

7 The Queen was staying at Treetops, a hunting lodge near Mount Kenya, when she heard of her father's death.

8 King George VI and his family used HMS *Vanguard,* Britain's last battleship, for the Royal tour of South Africa in 1946-47.

9 King Henry VIII was thrown by Francis, King of France, at the Field of the Cloth of Gold in 1520.

10 The Queen has flown at least twice in Concorde – once on her return from Barbados in 1977 ; and, later, when travelling to the Middle East in 1979.

11 The Queen met Fletcher Christian's descendant when she landed at Suva in the Fiji Islands during the tour of the Commonwealth in 1953-54.

12 During the same tour, the Queen said this to the New Zealand Prime Minister, when he draped a plastic raincoat over her shoulders during a sudden shower.

Medals and decorations

1 What award for valour may have been designed by a Royal – and from what is it still manufactured?

2 How many investitures are held each year – when the Queen (or, in her absence, another member of the Royal Family) personally presents the awards?

3 What are the surviving orders of chivalry in Britain?

4 Most of the civil awards are made on the recommendation of the Government, but there is one Order which is at the discretion of the Sovereign – for personal services to the Monarch or to members of the Royal Family. Which?

5 What Orders and medals does the Queen wear at Trooping the Colour?

6 The motto of the Order of the Garter is *Honi Soit qui mal y Pense*. How did it originate?

7 With whose sword did the Queen confer a knighthood upon Francis Chichester after his single-handed circum-navigation of the globe?

8 Upon what non-person may James I have conferred a knighthood?

9 What Orders does the Duke of Edinburgh wear around his neck?

10 One of the Orders that has been conferred upon the Queen has some connection with an elephant. What is it – and from what country did it come?

11 What is the most recent Order of Chivalry?

12 Most of the Orders are divided up into different classes. What are they?

13 What Second World War campaign medals does the Duke of Edinburgh wear?

Answers **Royal shopping**

1   Donald Campbell, from whom the Princess of Wales has bought dresses, was given cut-outs of two American comic-strip characters when he was eight. To increase their wardrobes, he made additional clothes for them.

2   Sir Norman Hartnell.

3   Lord Mountbatten introduced the Prince of Wales to Turnbull & Asser in London's Jermyn Street.

4   Queen Victoria was once depicted drinking cocoa in a train – with Windsor Castle in the background. The advertisement was the work of Cadbury. Nowadays, such impertinence would never be allowed.

5   The common factor is Burberrys Limited.

6   At least £8.50. The hairdresser, incidentally, is Geo. F. Trumper of Curzon Street, London.

7   The sword maker in all probability would be Wilkinson Sword Limited. A knighthood may be too much to hope for, but they make razors and razor blades as well.

8   The kennels that accommodate the Queen's labradors at Sandring-ham and the gun-dogs at Balmoral are a foot larger than standard. They are manufactured by a firm near Peterborough.

9   Elizabeth Arden was training to be a nurse when she decided to leave Canada and seek work in a New York beauty salon.

10   Benson and Hedges Limited in Old Bond Street. The King knew them well – they supplied his cigars.

11   Kimbolton Fireworks, suppliers of pyrotechnics to Royalty and gentry, was founded by a clergyman.

12   James Lock & Company – to some people, the *only* hatters. Anyone wanting a similar polo helmet should ask for a 'polo cap HRH pattern'. Prince Charles gets his there, too.

13   Mr Thomas Joy, managing director of Hatchards Limited in Piccadilly.

14   David and Elizabeth Emanuel – a young West End couple brilliantly dressing a young Princess. The public loved the idea.

15   Earl Grey.

Answers   Medals and decorations

1   Prince Albert may have had a hand in the design of the Victoria Cross (though there is a mystery about this). The medals are manufactured by Handcocks & Company of London – from bronze taken from Russian canons captured at Sevastopol. The Department of Defence has charge of the supply. So seldom is the VC awarded, that there is still plenty of raw material left.

2   Fourteen. Those held at Buckingham Palace take place in the Ball Room.

3   The Most Noble Order of the Garter, The Most Ancient and Most Noble Order of the Thistle, The Most Honourable Order of the Bath, The Most Distinguished Order of St Michael and St George, The Royal Victorian Order, and The Most Excellent Order of the British Empire.

4   The Royal Victorian Order.

5   The Garter, CI (Imperial Order of the Crown of India), the Defence Medal (1939-1945), the War Medal (1939-1945), King George V Jubilee Medal, King George VI Coronation Medal, and the Canadian Forces Decoration.

6   The Order of the Garter probably originated at a ball held in Calais to celebrate the town's capture in 1347. Joan, the Fair Maid of Kent (the Black Prince was her second husband), dropped a blue garter when dancing. The King (Edward III) picked it up.

When some people jeered, he put it on his own leg – saying (to translate) 'Shame on him who thinks evil of it.'

7   Sir Francis Drake's.

8   James I (according to one story) was dining at a house in Lancashire. The loin of beef was so good that he drew his sword and 'thrice imposed the knightly slap' – dubbing it 'Sir Loin'.

9   The Order of Merit and the Order of the British Empire – Grand Master.

10   In 1947, the Queen (then Princess Elizabeth) was awarded the Order of the Elephant by the King of Denmark.

11   The Most Excellent Order of the British Empire was created by George V on 17 June 1917. The object was to reward civilians for their services to Britain and the Commonwealth during the First World War.

12   Apart from the Garter and the Thistle (which have only one rank) the Orders are divided up into five classes: Knights or Dames Grand Cross, Knights or Dames Commander, Companions or Commanders, Officers, and Members.

13   The Duke of Edinburgh has them all: the 1939-1945 Star, the Atlantic Star, the Burma Star with Pacific Rosette, and the Italy Star. He was also awarded the Greek War Cross, and the Croix de Guerre with Laurel.

Royal finances

1 What is the difference between the Civil List and the Privy Purse?

2 What annual income does the Prince of Wales receive from the Civil List?

3 How much does it cost the nation to maintain the Royal Family for one year?

4 Where and when did Prince Philip say that the Monarchy would soon be 'in the red'?

5 At the beginning of the Queen's reign, the Civil List income was set at £475,000. It had not been increased since . . . when?

6 In 1982, how much did the Queen receive from the Civil List?

7 Does the Queen pay rates?

8 How much does the Queen pay annually on wages and salaries?

9 In what year did the Civil List expenditure exceed its income for the first time in modern history?

10 What does the word 'Civil' in Civil List imply?

11 Who receives payments from the Civil List?

12 What is the Duke of Edinburgh's annual income from the state?

13 When the Queen goes abroad, does she have to pay duty on any purchases she may have made?

14 Payments to three members of the Royal Family from the Civil List are refunded by the Queen. Who are they?

15 Who are the Queen's bankers?

Answers   Royal finances

NOTE: Where sums of money are given, they are up to date at the time of writing. However, they will almost certainly be more by the time this book appears. Thus readers, when checking their answers, are asked to make allowances for this.

1   The Civil List is money paid by the state to the Royal Family under an Act of Parliament. It should not be confused with the Privy Purse, which is concerned with the Queen's personal expenditure and is fed from the Queen's private income. For example, the upkeep of Buckingham Palace and Windsor Castle (the Sovereign's official residences) comes from the Civil List – whilst the Privy Purse is responsible for Sandringham and Balmoral (i.e. her private homes).

2   The Prince of Wales receives no income from the Civil List. The bulk of his money comes from the revenues of the Duchy of Cornwall. He surrenders a quarter of the amount to the Exchequer by way of tax, and keeps the rest (in 1982, he kept £600,000).

3   Over £15 million.

4   Prince Philip said that 'next year we will be in the red' when interviewed on American TV in 1969. As a result, Parliament set up a Select Committee to look into the matter.

5   It had not been increased since the accession of Edward VII in 1901.

6   £3,850,000 (in 1984).

7   The Queen pays rates on her private houses – i.e. Balmoral and Sandringham.

8   The last available figure, published more than ten years ago, was £2,330,000. It may be less now, since economies have been introduced – e.g. the introduction of a word processor at Buckingham Palace.

9   In 1962 inflation overtook the Civil List payments.

10   The word 'Civil' was introduced during the reign of William and Mary as a reminder that – whilst the Sovereign still paid the officers of state, the judges, the ambassadors, and the civil service – Parliament paid the armed forces.

11   The Queen; the Queen Mother; the Duke of Edinburgh; Prince Andrew; Prince Edward; Princess Margaret; Princess Alice, Duchess of Gloucester; the Duke of Gloucester; the Duke of Kent; and Princess Alexandra. Prince Edward receives the least – £20,000 a year.

12   £186,500.

13   On return from abroad, the Queen pays duty on any purchases she may have made, but official gifts are exempted. (She does not, incidentally, require a passport.)

14   The Civil List payments to the Duke of Gloucester, the Duke of Kent, and Princess Alexandra (together, in 1984, they shared £331,000) are refunded by the Queen.

15   Coutts & Co in the Strand. With the exception of Edward VII, they have been bankers to the Sovereign since the reign of George IV. Edward VII banked with a firm in Whitehall that is now a branch of Barclays.

Royal shopping

1 What dressmaker to a Royal began to design clothes at the age of eight?

2 What Royal couturier received a knighthood?

3 Who introduced the Prince of Wales to his shirtmaker?

4 What Royal was depicted in an advertisement for what?

5 What makers of waterproofs to the Queen and to the Queen Mother provided garments for Captain R.F. Scott on his journey to the South Pole; for Alcock when he made the first non-stop transatlantic flight with Brown; and manufactured the raincoat Lord Kitchener was wearing when he died after HMS *Hampshire* struck a mine in 1916?

6 What is the least it would cost a man to have his hair cut at the establishment which groomed King George V from 1919 until his death in 1936?

7 Who manufactured the sword which the Sovereign uses when conferring a knighthood?

8 What kind of accommodation supplied to the Queen is one foot longer than standard size?

9 What supplier of cosmetics to Royalty began her career by becoming a student nurse?

10 To what shop did Edward VII, after being given a sample of tobacco by the Egyptian government, take it and order it to be made up into cigarettes?

11 What firm, supplying what festive delights to the Royal Family, was founded by a vicar, who is still its top man?

12 What firm produced a fibreglass polo helmet for the Duke of Edinburgh?

13 What bookseller is a Member of the Royal Victorian Order, and runs a shop that dates back to 1797?

14 Who designed and manufactured the Princess of Wales's wedding dress?

15 To what kind of tea is the Queen partial?

The name game

Each of the following is (or, if deceased, was) a member of the Royal Family. Readers are invited to decide who they are. To make it more difficult, one name has been omitted in every case. It is, of course, the one by which they are more commonly known.

1   Alexandra Mary.

2   Charles Albert David.

3   Frances.

4   Elizabeth Alice Louise.

5   Arthur Philip.

6   Angela Marguerite.

7   Philip Arthur George.

8   Edward Nicholas Paul Patrick.

9   Albert Christian Edward.

10 Albert Frederick Arthur.

11 Antony Richard Louis.

12 Helen Elizabeth Olga Christabel.

13 Albert Christian George Andrew Patrick David.

14 Anthony Peter.

1 HM The Queen.
2 Prince Harry.
3 The Princess of Wales.
4 Princess Anne.
5 Prince William.
6 HM The Queen Mother.
7 The Prince of Wales.
8 The Duke of Kent.
9 Prince Andrew.
10 King George VI.
11 Prince Edward.
12 Princess Alexandra.
13 King Edward VIII (The Duke of
   Windsor).
14 Captain Mark Phillips.

Royal ancestors

1 The Queen's ancestry can be traced back to William the Conqueror. Why does this suggest that the British Royal Family has Scandinavian origins?

2 Chance (or fate?) has much to do with the making of history. Had it not been for the deaths of three women in the early nineteenth century, Elizabeth II might not be Queen today. Who were those women?

3 What is the relationship of George III to the present Queen?

4 What law still makes it impossible for anyone who is a Roman Catholic – or who marries one – to become the Sovereign of Britain?

5 Who was the first Monarch to marry a commoner?

6 Who was the first Sovereign to have a marriage annulled?

7 George I was the Elector of Hanover – in other words, a German. Did he need to become naturalized before taking over the throne of England?

8 Which ancestor of a present-day Royal found it necessary to change his name?

9 Which King in the past 200 years was succeeded by his brother?

10 Prince Charles is the . . . Prince of Wales. (Or, to put it another way, how many Princes of Wales had there been before his investiture?)

11 To show their Scottish connections, the Queen (and members of her family) often wear kilts when at Balmoral. What tartans can they use?

12 What Sovereign had five children – and outlived them all?

13 Not all Princes of Wales have succeeded to the throne. How many did not?

14 William III belonged to the House of Orange in the Netherlands. What qualifications did he have to become King of England?

Answers Royal ancestors

1   William was Duke of Normandy, and Normandy did not belong to the King of France. In the ninth century, it was frequently attacked by the Norsemen who, by the early tenth century, had established themselves in the area.

2   Princess Charlotte (daughter of George IV), another Princess Charlotte and Princess Elizabeth (both daughters of William IV). Had they not died, Victoria would have been unlikely to have come to the throne.

3   If he were alive, George III would be the Queen's great-great-great-great grandfather.

4   The Act of Settlement 1701.

5   Henry IV married Mary Bohun, but she never became Queen.

6   King John's marriage to Isobel, Countess of Gloucester, was annulled in 1200 – the year after John came to the throne.

7   No: George I's mother, Sophia – the Electress of Hanover – had already had British nationality and Royal status bestowed upon her by the Act of Settlement. The object was to block the way for a Roman Catholic to accede to the throne.

8   The Duke of Edinburgh's grandfather, Prince Louis of Battenberg, changed his name to Mountbatten during the First World War. Battenberg was too Germanic.

9   George IV was succeeded by his brother, William IV.

10   Prince Charles is the twenty-first Prince of Wales.

11   The Queen and her family have a choice of three tartans: the Royal Stewart, the Hunting Stewart, and the Balmoral (red and grey – it was designed by Prince Albert).

12   Queen Anne.

13   Five Princes of Wales never came to the throne. With the exception of James II's son, 'The Old Pretender', they died too soon.

14   William, Prince of Orange's grandfather was Charles I. His wife, Mary, was the daughter of James II. Thus they may be said to have had equal rights; and, as a result, they ruled jointly (in other words, Mary was not Queen Consort; but, as her husband, a reigning Monarch).

Royalty and charity

A privately printed book, giving details of the Royal Family's involvement in charities, runs to some 150 pages. Thus, the scale is enormous and it is impossible to provide more than a small sample in these pages. The following questions are taken more or less at random.

1 Who is Patron of the Leonard Cheshire Foundation?

2 Who is Patron of VSO (Voluntary Service Overseas)?

3 Who is Patron of MIND (The National Association for Mental Health)?

4 Who is President of the NSPCC (National Society for the Prevention of Cruelty to Children)?

5 Who is President of the Marie Curie Memorial Foundation, which gives services to cancer patients?

6 Who are Patrons of the RNLI?

7 Who is President of Save the Children?

8 Who is Patron of the British Paraplegic Sports Society?

9 Who is Patron of the Jubilee Sailing Trust (an organization that teaches the disabled how to sail)?

10 Who is Patron of the Royal School for the Blind?

11 Who is President of the National Playing Fields Association?

12 Who is International President of the World Wildlife Fund?

Answers   Royalty and charity

1   The Queen – she gave Park House
    at Sandringham to the Foundation
    for use as one of its homes.

2   The Duke of Edinburgh.

3   Princess Alexandra.

4   Princess Margaret.

5   The Queen Mother.

6   The Queen and the Queen Mother.

7   Princess Anne.

8   The Prince of Wales.

9   Prince Andrew.

10   The Princess of Wales.

11   The Duke of Edinburgh.

12   The Duke of Edinburgh.

Royalty and railways

1   When did the present Royal train come into service?

2   Is a special engine-driver allocated for duty with the Royal train?

3   What are the colours of the Royal train's carriages?

4   When did a British Sovereign travel by rail for the first time – and over what distance?

5   Which King, when asked about the design for a new saloon, said, 'Make it like a yacht'?

6   The first long distance train journey by Royalty involved two overnight stops at hotels. Where were they?

7   Which British Sovereign had armour-plated coaches in his Royal train?

8   For whom was a special saloon coach kept at Calais?

9   Which railway company installed a fountain on the front of a locomotive to celebrate the coronations of Edward VII and George V?

10   Which Royal would never permit the engine-driver to exceed 40 mph (65 km/h)?

11   Which Royal, enjoying speed, instructed the driver of a new type of locomotive to 'Show me what it can do'?

12   What facility does the Royal train offer the Royal corgis?

13   For which Royal couple were baths first installed in a Royal train?

14   Who owns the Royal train?

Answers   Royalty and railways

1   The latest Royal rolling stock first came into service on 16 May 1977, when the Queen and the Duke of Edinburgh used the coaches for an overnight journey to Scotland.

2   No. There used to be an elite of drivers and guards ear-marked for Royal trains; but, nowadays, any 'top link' (BR's expression) man will do. Frequently, whoever is assigned to the task does not know who his passengers will be.

3   The carriages are painted in 'Royal claret'. In bad light, it could be mistaken for black.

4   On 13 June 1842, Queen Victoria travelled from Slough station (where a special Royal waiting-room had been built) to Paddington – a distance of 18¼ miles (nearly 30 km).

5   King Edward VII.

6   The journey was from Aberdeen to Euston in 1848, and Queen Victoria was the Royal passenger. It had to be arranged at the last minute, when bad weather suggested that it might be dangerous to use the Royal Yacht. On the first night, the Queen stayed at the George (now Royal George) Hotel at Perth; on the second, at the Royal Hotel, Crewe.

7   King George VI. The armour-plating was a precaution against air attack in the Second World War.

8   The coach was kept at Calais for Queen Victoria, when she travelled on holiday to her villa near Cannes.

9   The London, Tilbury and South-end Railway. On each occasion, there were also busts of the newly enthroned King and Queen – one above each buffer, with the fountain playing in the middle.

10   Queen Victoria mistrusted speed.

11   Edward VII enjoyed it. The locomotive was the latest Atlantic type to enter service with the LNER.

12   A piece of carpet upon which they can make themselves comfort-able. When not in use, it is kept in the Royal Trains store at Wolverton, Bucks.

13   Baths were first installed for King George V and Queen Mary – when the extra travelling incurred by the First World War meant that the Royal train would sometimes virtually become a Royal home. The present Royal train has a bath for the Queen and a shower compartment for Prince Philip.

14   British Rail owns the Royal train.

A batch of bloomers

1   Who, when opening a new annexe to a public building, suffered a lapse of memory, and said, 'I declare this thing open – whatever it is'?

2   Who conferred so many knighthoods that he was unable to recall the names of those whom he was honouring; and, consequently, had to mumble, 'Arise, Sir What-You-Will'?

3   What Royal mistook a tree in Windsor Park for the King of Prussia?

4   What visiting Royal (and when) was kept waiting in his London hotel, when he should have been at Saint James's Palace?

5   Who, in a case of mistaken identity, told a Royal to 'get the hell out of it'?

6   What Sovereign caused angry murmurings among the crew of the Royal Yacht by inadvertently preventing them from having their rum rations?

7   Which Sovereign was tricked by one of his courtiers into conferring fraudulent knighthoods?

8   Which Sovereign made the serious mistake of suspecting that an unmarried lady-in-waiting was pregnant – when, in fact, she was suffering from a tumour on the liver?

9   Whose consort was tricked into shouting at a guest (and the guest into shooting at her), when each was told that the other was deaf?

10 Which Sovereign's conduct caused a critic to erect the following notice outside Buckingham Palace: 'These commanding premises to be let or sold in consequence of the late occupant's declining business'?

Answers   A batch of bloomers

1   The Duke of Edinburgh when opening a new annexe to Vancouver City Hall in 1969. Since then, it has been known as 'the East Thing'.

2   James I on his progress from Edinburgh to London on the occasion of his accession to the English throne. He conferred 133 knighthoods during the journey.

3   George III.

4   The Emperor of Russia was kept waiting at his hotel in 1814, when he came to London to attend celebrations marking the defeat of Napoleon and the French leader's exile to Elba. The Lord Chamberlain, who should have had matters in hand, was at Saint James's Palace – wondering what had become of the Emperor.

5   The Royal train had been shunted into a siding to ensure its occupants a good night's sleep. The Duke of Edinburgh rose early. He decided to take a short stroll and wandered over to a nearby signal box. The signalman said, 'It's as much as my job's worth to let you in here with all that lot down below. Just you get the hell out of it.'

6   Queen Victoria's chair was blocking the door to the place where the rum was kept. Her Majesty agreed to move on condition that she might have a tot. Afterwards, she said, 'I think it would be very good if it were stronger'.

7   George IV. A Lord-in-Waiting was fooled by two fraudulent characters into admitting them to an investiture. The truth was discovered; but, said one newspaper, 'These two knights, we understand, cannot be unknighted'.

8   Queen Victoria. The Lady-in-Waiting was Lady Flora Hastings. The villain was Sir James Clark, the court doctor. Queen Victoria had considerable faith in him – though his powers of diagnosis left a good deal to be desired.

9   The wife of Edward IV, Elizabeth Wydville, was tricked by her husband's jester – a man named Scoggin. The other lady was Mrs Scoggin.

10   Queen Victoria. The notice was put up after, in the view of many people, she had retired from public life for too long following the death of Prince Albert.

Royal customs

1 Trooping the Colour takes place on the Queen's *official* birthday. Why does she have two birthdays?

2 On a number of specified days, Royal Salutes are fired by the King's Troop of the Royal Horse Artillery and by the Honourable Artillery Company. Among them are certain birthdays. Whose birthdays?

3 What is the origin of firing guns as a salute?

4 What ceremony do the Yeomen of the Guard perform on the eve of the State Opening of Parliament?

5 On Maundy Thursday (i.e. the Thursday before Easter) the Queen dispenses sums of money. How much money is involved, and how many people receive it?

6 As recently as the mid-nineteenth century, the killing of a certain kind of bird was punishable by deportation for seven years. What kind of bird?

7 Only certain regiments are permitted to beat their drums in the City of London. Which regiments?

8 When the Sovereign enters the City of London, the Lord Mayor surrenders an object to her. What is this object?

9 When the Queen made her progress along the Thames as part of the 1977 Silver Jubilee celebrations, she was accompanied by a man who had been world Professional Sculling Champion from 1928 to 1930. Who was he?

10 The Queen's mount at Trooping the Colour is a horse named Burmese. Who gave Burmese to Her Majesty?

11 What is the origin of the bearskins worn by the Queen's footguards?

12 An annual event on the Thames is known as the Doggett's Coat and Badge Race. It was originally organized to celebrate a Royal birthday. Whose birthday – and who was Doggett?

13 When the Sovereign arrives in Edinburgh to stay at Holyrood House, she is presented with the keys of the city. How old are they?

Answers   Royal customs

1   Trooping the Colour was first carried out to celebrate the Sovereign's (George III) birthday in 1805. It became a tradition and, until Edward VII, subsequent Monarchs had conveniently been born during the summer months. But Edward VII arrived in November – when the weather bodes ill for such a ceremony. Consequently, he decided to have an *official* birthday in June, when the sun might shine on the parade.

2   The birthdays of the Queen (her real one and her official one), the Duke of Edinburgh, and of the Queen Mother are all celebrated by the firing of Royal Salutes.

3   Just as a salute by hand shows that it conceals no weapon, so does the firing of a cannon (in this case a 13-pounder gun) show that its content had been discharged and that, unless it is reloaded, it cannot be fired again.

4   The Yeomen of the Guard carry out a search of the cellars in the Houses of Parliament. The custom dates back to the Gunpowder Plot.

5   Maundy money is given to the deserving poor (until the reign of James II, the Sovereign used to wash their feet as well). The Queen hands each recipient two purses. One contains a Maundy shilling for every year of the Monarch's reign; the other, a penny for every year of the Monarch's life. The number of people to receive them adds up to the years of the Sovereign's life. Despite their

unique designs, the coins are legal tender – though the favoured few understandably prefer not to spend them.

6   A swan – which has always been regarded as a Royal bird and the property of the Sovereign.

7   The Blues and Royals, the Honourable Artillery Company, the Grenadier Guards, the Coldstream Guards, The Queen's Regiment, The Royal Regiment of Fusiliers, and the Royal Marines.

8   The Lord Mayor surrenders his sword. The Monarch used to take it over; but, since the reign of Charles I, he or she has only touched it and then returned it.

9   Albert Barry – the Royal Barge-master.

10   Burmese was a gift from the Royal Canadian Mounted Police, made to Her Majesty in 1969.

11   Bearskins were originally worn in the late eighteenth century – to make the soldiers look taller and more ferocious. They were first used for ceremonial parades in 1832.

12   The birthday was George I's (1 August); Doggett was an Irish comedian; the race takes place over a 4½-mile stretch of the Thames.

13   The present keys to the city of Edinburgh are more than 350 years old. They were manufactured for a visit by Charles I in 1629.

Royal servants

1   What Royal servant gained his appointment by standing under a water spout for several hours?

2   Who are Miss Barnes and Miss Lightbody?

3   What Royal servant later disgraced herself by writing a column in a popular women's magazine?

4   What Royal servant received a gold medal and an annuity of £25 for helping to overpower a would-be assassin?

5   Who is 'Bobo' MacDonald?

6   What duties do the Pages of the Back Stairs perform?

7   At what alarming incident was a girl named Elizabeth Andrew present?

8   What Sovereign invited his host's cook to stay at Buckingham Palace?

9   What Sovereign ordered all his kitchen staff to have their heads shaven?

10 What governess gained so much influence over her charge that, later on, she was given a title and entrusted with handling the Privy Purse?

Answers   Royal servants

1   A man named Scoggin accepted a bet of £20 that he would not stand under a water spout for a longish period. Towards the end of his ordeal, and dreadfully wet, he was noticed by Edward IV. The King decided that anyone so foolish would make a good jester – and offered Scoggin the job.

2   Miss Barnes is nanny to Prince William; Miss Lightbody was nanny to the Prince of Wales.

3   Marion Crawford (or 'Crawfie') was governess to Princess Elizabeth and Princess Margaret Rose. After relinquishing the appointment in the late 1940s, she took to writing books and articles.

4   Queen Victoria's John Brown. Acting with Prince Arthur, Duke of Connaught, he overpowered a Fenian (a forerunner of the IRA) named Arthur O'Connor. O'Connor was about to point a pistol at Queen Victoria – which, by some apparent oversight, he had not loaded.

5   'Bobo' MacDonald – or Margaret MacDonald – has been the Queen's dresser since 1952. She joined the Royal Family in 1926 as nursery maid to Princess Elizabeth.

6   They attend on the Queen and Prince Philip.

7   Miss Andrew came into the Queen's bedroom after an unemployed labourer named Michael Fagan had broken into it during the early morning of a day in 1982. She is reputed to have said, 'Ooh, bloody 'ell, Ma'am, what's 'e doing 'ere?'

8   King Edward VII was so impressed by the cuisine of Mrs Baker, cook to Admiral of the Fleet Lord Fisher, that he invited her to Buckingham Palace to see how a Great State Dinner was managed.

9   George III. There was industrial unrest among the palace servants: it reached its nadir when a louse was discovered on the King's plate at dinner. All the kitchen staff submitted to the indignity of having their heads shaven – with the exception of one youth, who was dismissed.

10   The future Queen Victoria's governess, Louise Lehzen, who later became Baroness Lehzen. She was a clergyman's daughter from Hanover.

Royalty and the media

1 Which Sovereign took the unprecedented step of writing a letter for publication in what newspaper?

2 When was the first broadcast made by a member of the Royal Family?

3 Who sprayed press photographers with paint?

4 Prince Philip, when guest at a luncheon given by industrial editors, told them that the Royal Family has its own house magazine. To what was he referring?

5 Who introduced Edward VIII when he faced up to a microphone to make his abdication broadcast?

6 The former husband of which Royal was employed by which Sunday newspaper?

7 Which peer of the realm wrote a scathing attack on the Monarchy in a monthly review?

8 A journalist spent a year in jail for libelling which Royal?

9 Who said to radio listeners, 'I dedicate myself anew to your service for all the years that may still be given me.'?

10 Who directed a TV documentary about the life of the Royal Family – and what was its title?

11 Who said of press photographers, 'All those chaps ever want is the moment when they catch you picking your nose'?

12 What newspaper owner suggested that Buckingham Palace should be used as a home for 'fallen women'?

13 What newspaper editor did the Queen accuse of having made 'an exceedingly pompous remark'?

14 To whom was this New York newspaper headline referring: 'Here he is, girls – the most eligible bachelor yet uncaught'?

15 An American journalist once wrote: 'It should be understood that when . . . is on . . . travels considerably less ceremonial is observed than when the Court is in England or Scotland'. Who was the traveller?

Answers **Royalty and the media**

1   The letter, which was unsigned, was written by Queen Victoria to *The Times*, explaining (or excusing?) her absence from public life after the death of Prince Albert.

2   The Prince of Wales (later Edward VIII) made an address to a rally of Boy Scouts on 7 October 1922. It was transmitted by the station 2LO. The first broadcast by a reigning Sovereign was made by King George V on 23 April 1924, when the Empire Exhibition at Wembley was opened.

3   Prince Andrew.

4   The Court Circular.

5   Lord Reith, Director-General of the BBC.

6   Lord Snowdon, former husband of Princess Margaret, who was employed by the *Sunday Times*.

7   Lord Altrincham took a nasty swipe at the Royal Family in the August 1957 issue of the *National and English Review*. The article was widely quoted by the more popular press.

8   Shortly after his accession to the throne, King George V was libelled by a journalist named Edward Mylius. Mylius was prosecuted and sentenced to twelve months in prison.

9   King George V on the occasion of his Silver Jubilee. It was a sad promise: he died in the following year.

10   Richard Cawston. The film, appropriately, was entitled *Royal Family*. It was shown in 130 countries.

11   Prince Philip.

12   Henry Labouchère, owner of *Truth*. Labouchère was furious with Queen Victoria for having dissuaded Gladstone from giving him a post in the Cabinet.

13   A former editor of the *News of the World*. He had made some daft remark about Princess Diana sending 'a servant to get her sweeties' from the village shop.

14   The Prince of Wales (later Edward VIII, later Duke of Windsor) when he visited New York in 1924.

15   The missing words are 'the Queen' and 'her' – and the answer is: Queen Victoria.

Royalty in and out of danger

1 What Sovereign was kidnapped by a former ally?

2 Which Royal survived a kidnap attempt – though a policeman was wounded in the fracas?

3 Which Royal's father, under sentence of death, was rescued by a British cruiser?

4 Which Royal, when making a parachute jump, found that his feet were caught up in the shrouds?

5 How many attempts were there on the life of Queen Victoria?

6 During a Royal visit to an industrial undertaking, a bomb exploded in the power house. Who was the Royal, and where did the incident take place?

7 Who was where when (in his words) 'We see the soldiers going up and down, in the thicket of a wood, searching for prisoners escaped'?

8 What Royal was fortunate to survive when his ship was sunk by enemy aircraft in the Second World War?

9 What caused Winston Churchill to snarl, 'Is it your intention to wipe out the Royal Family in the shortest possible time'?

10 Which Royal manned a searchlight during the Battle of Matapan in the Second World War?

11 What Royal was shot at through the open window of his railway compartment when the train was about to depart from Brussels?

12 When was an object hurled at the Sovereign during Trooping the Colour – and who was the Sovereign?

Answers   **Royalty in and out of danger**

1   Richard I was kidnapped by Duke Leopold of Austria when returning from a crusade. Eventually he was released on payment of a £100,000 ransom.

2   One evening in 1974, Princess Anne and Captain Mark Phillips were returning along the Mall to Buckingham Palace. A man, who was later detained under the Mental Health Act, rammed the car and opened fire. The couple's police bodyguard was wounded. Both the Princess and her husband escaped unharmed.

3   Prince Philip's father, Prince Andrew of Greece, was charged with treason by the Greek government in 1922. He would certainly have been shot, had it not been for British intervention and the timely arrival of the cruiser HMS *Calypso*.

4   Prince Charles. He described it as 'a rather hairy experience'.

5   Six – they all took place on informal occasions in the streets of London.

6   The Queen was opening the oil terminal at Sullom Voe, Shetland, when a bomb exploded in the power house. It was some distance from Her Majesty, and nobody was hurt.

7   Charles II – when hiding in a bushy pollard oak situated in the Forest of Brewood, Shropshire.

8   Earl Mountbatten, when his destroyer, HMS *Kelly,* was sunk by German divebombers in the Mediterranean. More than half the *Kelly*'s crew were killed.

9   Churchill growled these words when Prince Philip's private secretary informed him that HRH proposed to learn to fly helicopters.

10   Prince Philip was a midshipman in the battleship HMS *Valiant* when several Italian warships were wiped out at Matapan. He was mentioned in dispatches for his gallant conduct.

11   King Edward VII, when he was Prince of Wales. As he noted afterwards '. . . a man fires a pistol at P. of W. through open window of carriage (no harm done).'

12   At the 1936 Trooping the Colour, an Irishman threw a revolver in the direction of Edward VIII. He was jailed for one year.

Royal birthdays

Who was born on the following days:

1   19 May 1819.

2   3 June 1865.

3   14 December 1895.

4   4 August 1900.

5   10 June 1921.

6   21 April 1926.

7   21 August 1930.

8   22 September 1948.

9   14 November 1948.

10   15 August 1950.

11   19 February 1960.

12   1 July 1961.

13   10 March 1964.

14   21 June 1982.

15   15 September 1984.

Answers   Royal birthdays

1   Queen Victoria.
2   King George V.
3   King George VI.
4   Queen Elizabeth The Queen Mother.
5   Prince Philip, Duke of Edinburgh.
6   HM The Queen.
7   Princess Margaret.
8   Captain Mark Phillips.
9   The Prince of Wales.
10 Princess Anne.
11 Prince Andrew.
12 The Princess of Wales.
13 Prince Edward.
14 Prince William.
15 Prince Harry.

Innovations

1   What Sovereign may have made a trip along the Thames in a submarine?

2   Who was the first Royal to ride a bicycle?

3   Which was the first British Queen to drive a car?

4   Who was the first Royal to attend a football match?

5   Which was the first Sovereign to go on a state visit?

6   Which was the first reigning Sovereign to visit the USA?

7   Which was the first Royal to attend an English prep school?

8   Who was the first member of the Royal Family to appear on TV?

9   Who was the first reigning Sovereign to make a non-stop long-distance flight?

10 Who was the first Royal to adopt a more informal style with the public?

11 Who was the first member of the Royal Family to take a job in commerce?

12 How did a Royal encourage the economic use of hot water?

Answers Innovations

1   In 1620, James I is said to have travelled in a submarine craft from Westminster to Greenwich. However, it is only fair to say that the evidence for this is far from substantial – though he certainly inspected the small vessel.

2   Prince Albert – in 1851.

3   Queen Alexandra (wife of Edward VII) had an electrically propelled car, which she drove with great panache on the estate at Sandringham.

4   The Prince of Wales (later Edward VII) attended the Gentlemen *v* Players match at the Oval in 1886. (No: this is not a misprint. The Oval doubled as a football ground for several years.)

5   King Henry VIII can be given credit for the first state visit by an English Monarch, when he produced the extravaganza known as the Field of the Cloth of Gold on French soil in 1520.

6   King George VI in 1939.

7   Prince Charles attended Hill House School in London; and, later, went as a border to Cheam School in Hampshire.

8   Princess Marina, Duchess of Kent, was seen on TV in 1935. Her Royal Highness was buying a hat in a London store at the time. Two years later, George VI was the first Monarch to be televised – as the coronation procession returned to Buckingham Palace.

9   King George VI. In 1943, he flew to North Africa in an Avro York – a four-engined aircraft that was normally at Winston Churchill's disposal.

10   Edward VIII as Prince of Wales liked to mix with people. On one occasion, he shook so many hands that his right hand became bruised, and he had to use his left.

11   Prince William of Gloucester joined a merchant bank in the City on 5 January 1965.

12   During the Second World War, King George VI had a line drawn on each bath in Buckingham Palace – five inches from the bottom. This marked the maximum permissible water level. The object, of course, was to save fuel.

Royal etiquette

1 At whose Court did Welshmen have to be instructed neither to strike the Queen nor to snatch anything from her?

2 What, in Georgian times, were forbidden to be worn at court – and, similarly, what minor physical afflictions were frowned upon?

3 In an attempt to tighten up etiquette at Queen Victoria's Court, Prince Albert ruled that men must not . . . in the Queen's presence – except at dinner. What is the missing word?

4 What was the rule in the nineteenth century that made it preferable to travel to Buckingham Palace in one type of conveyance rather than another?

5 How did a gentleman conduct himself on being presented to Queen Victoria at the Palace?

6 In speaking to the present Queen, how should one address her?

7 On being introduced to a member of the present Royal Family, what should one do?

8 How should a letter to the Queen begin – and how should it end?

9 If, in the nineteenth century, somebody found him or herself in the Royal presence and was uncertain of what to do, what was suggested as probably the best idea?

10 At whose Court was it considered bad form to take advantage of the mistletoe that adorned Windsor Castle at Christmas?

11 Who insisted that a courtier should not compete against a less exalted individual unless he was certain of winning?

12 Who used to walk through the public rooms of his residence late in the evening – counting the people present and making sure that nobody had gone to bed without his permission.

Answers   Royal etiquette

1   At the Court of the Anglo-Saxon Monarchs. The Welsh appear to have been an unruly people in those days. Since then, their manners have improved.

2   Spectacles – also sneezing and coughing.

3   The missing word is 'sit'. Even Disraeli had to observe the ordeal by standing when suffering from a bad attack of gout. The Queen followed her husband's example by making it plain that no maid of honour should sit in Prince Albert's presence – nor speak to him unless spoken to.

4   Anyone travelling in a coach could drive up to the doors of the Palace. Those who made the journey in hackney carriages had to disembark at the end of St James's Street – and walk the rest of the way.

5   He went down on one knee and raised his right arm with the back of his hand uppermost. The Queen then laid the palm of her hand upon it. Whereupon, he would brush it with his lips: rise, bow, and retire backwards. (To overdo the kissing bit was severely discouraged.)

6   In the beginning, the Queen should be addressed as 'Your Majesty' – thereafter as 'Ma'am' (to rhyme with Pam). Similarly with Princes and Princesses: initially 'Your Royal Highness' and afterwards 'Sir' or 'Ma'am' as the case may be.

7   On entering or leaving a Royal presence, men should bow – but using only the head (i.e. not from the waist). Women should curtsy.

8   The letter should begin with: Madam
With my humble duty,
And end:
I have the honour to remain,
   Madam,
      Your Majesty's most humble and
      obedient servant,
In the letter the words 'you' and 'your' should not be used. Instead, 'Your Majesty' and 'Your Majesty's' are preferred. But a better, and certainly less complicated, method is to write to 'The Private Secretary to Her Majesty The Queen'.

9   Stand to attention and say nothing – having first removed one's hat.

10   Queen Victoria's.

11   Henry VIII.

12   Edward VII.

Who said ?

1   'She means to be a Queen and not a puppet'.

2   'Do not I beseech you try to do any *good*; then at least you may be sure you do no harm'.

3   'I may be uninspiring, but I'll be damned if I am alien'.

4   'I never felt so sorry for anyone in all my life. He looked as if you'd dropped half the world on him'.

5   'Would you marry an American girl if you fell in love with one?'

6   'Why don't my Ministers talk to me as the President did tonight? I feel exactly as though a father was giving me his most careful and wise advice'.

7   'Oh ma'am, they are everywhere. I find it so off-putting'.

8   'I think everyone will concede that today, of all occasions, I should begin my speech with "My husband and I" '.

9   'How would you react to the suggestion that the Zoo could be run more cheaply if the exhibits were all stuffed animals?'

10 'I had hoped for something more original from the Prince of Wales'.

11 'My father was frightened of his mother, I was frightened of my father, and I am damned well going to see that my children are frightened of me'.

12 'I don't think people mind a little downright rudeness or prejudice. They excuse all that provided the person actually does the stuff they expect him to do'.

Answers Who said?

1 Harold MacMillan on the accession of Queen Elizabeth II.

2 Lord Melbourne, when Prime Minister. He was advising the young Queen Victoria.

3 King George V – referring to his Hanoverian ancestry when anti-German feeling was sweeping Britain in the First World War. Shortly afterwards, the name of the British Royal Family was changed to Windsor.

4 Prince Philip's private secretary, Lieutenant-Commander Michael Parker, describing the Prince's reactions to the news that King George VI had died.

5 The question was put to the Prince of Wales (later Edward VIII) during his visit to America in 1924. The Prince's answer was 'Yes'.

6 King George VI reflecting on his conversation with President Franklin D. Roosevelt in 1939.

7 Princess Diana, speaking to The Queen about the invasion of her life by press photographers.

8 The Queen – talking of the speech she proposed to make on the occasion of her Silver Wedding in November 1972.

9 Prince Philip – countering an argument that, instead of preserving certain ships that had historic importance, models would suffice.

10 The Duchess of Windsor (then Mrs Simpson) on meeting her future husband for the first time.

11 King George V.

12 Prince Philip.

Royalty and showbiz

1   Who, later to become well known as an actress, became the mistress of which Royal in 1877?

2   Which Royal played the title role in *Macbeth* – whereas, earlier on but in similar circumstances, his father had performed a lesser part in the same play?

3   Queen Elizabeth II is known to share with her great-great-grandmother, Queen Victoria, a fondness for the works of a famous writer-composer team. Who are they?

4   What was the first feature film to be shown by Royal Command?

5   Which Royal was once pelted with pork pies on the stage?

6   Who was the first member of the Royal Family to be portrayed on the stage during his/her lifetime?

7   Who was given fourteen days in which to write what play – at the behest of the reigning Sovereign?

8   What was the first film to be shown at a Royal Command Performance held in a public cinema?

9   Who played the part of Edward VIII in what popular TV series?

10 Which Royal made his/her TV debut in *Blue Peter*?

11 Which Royal appeared in the BBC's *Desert Island Discs* and included 'Rule Britannia' in his/her selection?

12 Which Sovereign liked a play to have a good plot, and enjoyed farce – provided it was not too bawdy?

13 Who delighted audiences of pensioners with his rendering of Glen Miller's *Chattanooga Choo Choo*?

Answers   Royalty and showbiz

1   Lillie Langtry became the mistress of the Prince of Wales (later Edward VII) in 1877. Strangely, neither the Princess of Wales nor Mr Langtry seem to have objected to the affair.

2   Prince Charles when at Gordonstoun. Prince Philip also performed in *Macbeth* at Gordonstoun, but he had to be content with the very much lesser part of Donalbain.

3   Gilbert and Sullivan.

4   *Comin' Through the Rye* was shown at Marlborough House, London, on 4 August 1916, on the instructions of Queen Alexandra (Edward VII's widow).

5   Prince Charles. It was no criticism of his performance: the role of the parson in Joe Orton's *Erpingham Camp* demanded it. HRH was up at Cambridge at the time: the production was staged by his college's dramatic society.

6   Queen Elizabeth the Queen Mother was portrayed as the Duchess of York in Royce Ryton's *Crown Imperial* in 1972. She was played by Amanda Reiss. The story centred around the Abdication crisis of 1936.

7   Shakespeare had two weeks in which to write *The Merry Wives of Windsor*. Queen Elizabeth was a great fan of Falstaff and she wanted more.

8   On 1 November 1946, *A Matter of Life and Death* (starring David Niven) was screened at the Empire, Leicester Square, before King George VI and his family.

9   Edward Fox in *Edward and Mrs Simpson*.

10   Princess Anne. The programme, which was screened in 1971, showed her touring the game parks of Kenya and also inspecting Save the Children activities. She was interviewed by Val Singleton.

11   Princess Margaret.

12   Queen Victoria.

13   Prince Edward. He and a few other Cambridge undergraduates formed a group to entertain pensioners and handicapped children.

Royalty and cars

1   Which was the first British Sovereign to own a motor car?

2   What make of car did the Sovereign use for important occasions until the designers drastically changed its shape?

3   What is the Queen's mascot?

4   What was the make of the car given by the RAF to Princess Elizabeth and Prince Philip as a wedding present – and thus began a new tradition?

5   How did a milk float solve a problem to do with the registration number of a Royal's car?

6   What member of the Royal Family holds a licence making it permissible to drive a heavy goods vehicle?

7   Who is in charge of the Queen's cars?

8   What make of car did King George VI prefer when he was Duke of York?

9   Who was the first Royal to have radio installed in a car?

10 Who, having made a short motor trip, received a letter from an aunt protesting, 'I very nearly had a fit and quite screamed out to myself . . . oh! dearest child, how could you?'?

11 What car did Princess Anne receive from her parents as an eighteenth birthday-present?

12 Are the Queen's cars required to carry number plates?

13 Where does the police bodyguard sit when he accompanies the Queen on car journeys?

14 What was the Prince of Wales's first car?

15 Has the Sovereign ever owned a second-hand car?

Answers   Royalty and cars

1   In 1900, Edward VII (then Prince of Wales) bought his first car – a Daimler.

2   Daimler. Its modern shape makes it unsuitable for ceremonial occasions.

3   Made from silver, it portrays a naked Saint George on a horse with a dead dragon underneath. In a sugar version, the design originally appeared on top of the Royal wedding cake in 1947.

4   The Royal Air Force gave Princess Elizabeth and Prince Philip a Rolls-Royce as a wedding present – and thus helped Rolls-Royce to usurp Daimler.

5   The milk float was discovered in Ealing. Its registration number was 1420H. The number was bought for Princess Anne by officers of the 14th/20th King's Hussars, of which she is Colonel-in-Chief.

6   Princess Anne.

7   The Crown Equerry, Lieutenant-Colonel Sir John Miller, KCVO, DSO, MC, who is in charge of the Royal Mews at Buckingham Palace.

8   A Lanchester – which, mechanically, was very similar to the Daimlers of its day.

9   On the urging of his family, King George VI. The set (a forerunner of today's transistors) was concealed in the arm rest; two loudspeakers were hidden in the bodywork behind the driver; and the aerial was installed beneath the running board.

10   Queen Mary when Duchess of York. The shocked correspondent was Augusta, Grand Duchess of Mecklenburg-Strelitz.

11   A Rover 2000TC.

12   The Rolls-Royces used for ceremonial occasions do not carry registration plates (though they have to be insured). The private cars belonging to the Royal Family must be registered, taxed and insured – just like those of other motorists.

13   In the Rolls-Royces, the police-man sits beside the chauffeur. In her private car, when the Queen is accompanied by Prince Philip, and Her Majesty is driving, he occupies the rear seat.

14   A cobalt blue MGC GT – bought in January 1968.

15   Yes – the second of the Rolls-Royces, a Phantom IV landaulette, was bought second hand.

Royalty and books

1   In what work of fiction did a Brigadier-General who, as a boy, was expelled from Rugby, and Edward VII appear in the same chapter?

2   Who wrote *Men, Machines, and Sacred Cows*?

3   Who said to whom: 'We authors, Ma'am'?

4   What is the title of the children's book written by Prince Charles?

5   *Banker* is the title of one work by an author the Queen enjoys; *The Mary Deare* is by another whose books she likes. Who are the two authors?

6   What was the book and who the author that Queen Victoria read to Prince Albert during his final illness?

7   Which author is godfather to a Prince?

8   Who wrote *Book of Sports*?

9   In what composition by a Royal author did the sentence 'War is, I fear, *quite* inevitable' appear?

10 Who compiled *A Guide to the Chatting Up of Girls*? And for whom?

11 Who wrote *A Question of Balance*?

12 Of what Royal was which Poet Laureate said to have written:

    Across the wires the electric message came:
    'He is no better, he is much the same'?

Answers Royalty and books

1 *Mr American* by George MacDonald Fraser. The Brigadier-General was Sir Harry Paget Flashman, VC, KCB, KCIE, etc. In this book, the notorious Flashman has what might be called a 'walk on' part.

2 The Duke of Edinburgh.

3 Disraeli to Queen Victoria after the latter's *Leaves from the Journal of Our Life in the Highlands* was published in 1868. He used the occasion to present the Queen with a complete set of his novels – written before he achieved success in politics.

4 *The Old Man of Lochnagar.*

5 Dick Francis (*Banker*) and Hammond Innes (*The Mary Deare*).

6 *Peveril of the Peak* by Sir Walter Scott.

7 Sir Laurens van der Post is godfather to Prince William.

8 James I. Published in 1618, it authorizes certain pastimes as suitable for the Sabbath. The London clergy disagreed.

9 *The Letters of Queen Victoria* – published in 1908. The 'war' she referred to was the Crimean.

10 The Prince of Wales. It is a German-English phrase book, written for the soldiers in the Royal Regiment of Wales, of which the Prince is Colonel-in-Chief.

11 The Duke of Edinburgh.

12 The lines are attributed to Alfred Austin – who succeeded Tennyson and held the post until his death in 1913. 'He' was the Prince of Wales (later Edward VII). Whilst the authorship may be uncertain, it would certainly not have been impossible for this rather indifferent poet to have written the jingle.

Royalty and sport

1   Which Royal captained a school hockey team?

2   Which Royal was captain of a golf club in Kent (a club, incidentally, of which James Bond's creator, Ian Fleming, became captain many years later)?

3   Who was the first Royal to attend an FA Cup Final?

4   Which Royal played tennis at Wimbledon?

5   Which Royal was unusually skilled at another kind of tennis – and built a court on which the game is still played?

6   For three generations, polo has been a favourite game of some Royals. How did it originate?

7   Which Royal had an unusual vehicle built in which to go grouse shooting?

8   Which Sovereign banned football on the grounds that it interfered with another sport that would be more useful in wartime?

9   Which Royal first experienced the pleasures of yacht racing?

10 Which Royal opened the present tennis courts at Wimbledon – and when?

Answers   Royalty and sport

1   The Princess of Wales. She was captain of the hockey team when a pupil at West Heath – a girls' public school near Sevenoaks in Kent.

2   The Prince of Wales (later Edward VIII) was captain of Royal St Georges golf club at Sandwich, Kent, in 1927/28. The Prince had a house nearby at Sandwich Bay.

3   George V attended the FA Cup Final at Wembley, when it was played there for the first time in 1923.

4   King George VI when he was Duke of York. He took part in a doubles match.

5   Henry VIII was adept at real tennis (sometimes called 'royal tennis' and sometimes, simply, 'tennis'. It is played on a larger court than lawn tennis and the rules are different.) He built the tennis court at Hampton Court in 1530.

6   Polo originated in India and was imported to Britain by cavalry officers in 1868. The name of the game is derived from *pulu,* a Tibetan word meaning 'ball'.

7   After his first serious illness, and aged 63, George V was too weak for the strenuous exercise of trudging over grouse moors. Nevertheless, his enthusiasm for the sport was undiminished. To enable him to enjoy it, a special six-wheeler car was built, which could travel across country. It was so designed that, if he wished, the King could shoot from its interior.

8   Richard II banned football. In those days, it was a game in which any number could play, and the antics of its players were, if anything, even more violent than those of today's soccer hooligans. The King's objection was that the time would be better spent practising archery.

9   Charles II was introduced to yacht racing while in exile in Holland. When he was restored to the throne of England, the Dutch East India Company presented him with a replica of a boat that he had particularly liked.

10   King George V – on 22 June 1922.

Royalty and aeroplanes

1 Who was the first Royal to take an interest in aircraft?

2 Who was the first Royal to qualify as a pilot?

3 Which Prince was rebuked by his father for having been flown over London by a pilot with an injured arm?

4 What gift did Prince Philip give the instructor who taught him to fly?

5 Who founded the Queen's Flight?

6 What is 'Purple Air Space'?

7 In 1984, plans were announced to introduce jet aircraft to the Queen's Flight. What type are they – and what were they intended to replace?

8 In what type of flying machine was a Captain of the Queen's Flight killed?

9 At what establishment was Prince Charles tested to discover whether he had the necessary aptitude to pilot an aircraft?

10 Where are the headquarters of the Queen's Flight?

11 What member of the Royal Family never uses a helicopter unless it is considered to be absolutely necessary?

12 Who was the first member of the Royal Family to land by helicopter on the deck of an aircraft carrier at sea?

13 Over what country were the Queen and the Duke of Edinburgh flying when, some years ago, they were 'buzzed' by fighters?

14 Is the use of aircraft in the Queen's Flight confined to members of the Royal Family?

15 What is the Prince of Wales's call sign – and what is Prince Philip's?

1   King Edward VII. In 1909, he motored from Biarritz to Pau, where he watched a demonstration by Wilbur Wright.

2   The future King George VI (then Prince Albert). He was awarded his wings on 31 July 1919.

3   The Prince of Wales (later Edward VIII). The pilot, a Canadian named Captain Barker, had flown the Prince over the Western Front in 1916. In 1918, one of his arms was damaged in a 'dog fight' over Northern Italy. He and his Royal passenger met again at a party in 1919. Barker suggested the trip: the Prince agreed at once.

4   A silver locket inscribed 'A reward for diligence'. Prince Philip said, 'You can use it to keep pills in'.

5   King Edward VIII. The King's Flight, as it then was, came into being on 20 July 1936.

6   Air space along the route of an aircraft in the Queen's Flight, which is kept free of traffic to make certain no mid-air collision occurs.

7   The HS146, which will replace the long outdated Andovers (powered by turbo-prop engines and having a cruising altitude of only 15,000 feet).

8   On 7 December 1967, Air Commodore John Blount was killed when the Whirlwind helicopter in which he was travelling crashed near a village in Berkshire. The main rotor shaft had snapped.

9   At RAF Tangmere, where an instructor from the Central Flying School took the Prince up in a Chipmunk.

10   RAF Benson in Oxfordshire.

11   The Queen.

12   The Queen Mother. Her Majesty was flown from her house at Birkhall near Balmoral and taken to HMS *Ark Royal,* which was in the Moray Firth. The date was 14 October 1975.

13   West Germany in November 1960. The Queen and her husband were returning in a Comet II from a visit to Denmark. According to the aircraft's co-pilot, the German fighters 'had damn great Iron Crosses underneath their wings'.

14   No. With the Queen's agreement, it can carry the Prime Minister, members of the government, service chiefs and visiting heads of state. In one year, it was estimated, 35 per cent of all its flights were made on behalf of non-Royals.

15   The Prince of Wales's call sign is 'Unicorn'; Prince Philip's, 'Rainbow'.

Royalty and politics

1 In 1689, the year in which William III and Mary II became jointly King and Queen, the Bill of Rights was passed by Parliament. In what ways did it curb the power of the Sovereign?

2 Who was the first Sovereign that did not preside over cabinet meetings?

3 Which Sovereign in the past 150 years insisted that all dispatches from the Foreign Office must be submitted for his/her approval – and sometimes re-wrote them?

4 Who was the last King to rule without Parliament?

5 According to Walter Bagehot in 1867 (and they apply just as much today), what three rights does the Sovereign still have?

6 Which Sovereign used to send which Prime Minister bunches of primroses from one of the Royal estates?

7 What unusual step did George V take in 1931?

8 What members of the Royal Household are political appointments?

9 Who was the last Sovereign to dismiss a government?

10 When did the Queen exercise the Royal Prerogative?

11 How many Prime Ministers have served under the present Queen?

12 To what leader of a Commonwealth country did the Queen send a sharp letter, reminding him of his duty to the Crown?

13 What are the 'red boxes'?

14 Does the Queen have a vote?

Answers   Royalty and politics

1   It forbade the Sovereign to suspend the law, to levy taxes, and to raise an army without the consent of Parliament.

2   George I – not least, because his command of English was so small. As a result, Robert Walpole (First Lord of the Treasury and Chancellor of the Exchequer) became what, to all intents and purposes, was the first Prime Minister.

3   Queen Victoria. The most famous example concerns the British ship *Trent*. During the American Civil War, it was stopped and boarded by a Federal (Northern) warship, and all the male passengers were taken off. On Palmerston's instructions, Lord Russell (the Foreign Secretary) drafted a dispatch that amounted to an ultimatum – release the captives, or else . . . It would probably have resulted in war between Britain and the Federal states, but Prince Albert toned it down. As a result, the captives were released and no shots were fired.

4   James II. Result: exile and his replacement by William of Orange and Mary.

5   According to Bagehot (an economist and journalist) the British Sovereign has 'the right to be consulted, the right to encourage, and the right to warn'.

6   Queen Victoria sent primroses to Disraeli. They were gathered by her Ladies-in-Waiting when she was at Osborne.

7   With Britain on the edge of bankruptcy, George V persuaded Prime Minister Ramsay MacDonald to form a coalition government. It was known as 'National Government'.

8   The Treasurer, the Comptroller, the Vice-Chamberlain, and six out of the eight Lords-in-Waiting are political appointments. The last of these are junior ministers in the House of Lords. Taking it in turns (for a month at a time), they represent the Sovereign at the arrival and departure of visiting heads of state, and on other special occasions.

9   William IV in 1834.

10   When Anthony Eden (later Lord Avon) resigned as Prime Minister on grounds of ill-health in 1957, there were two possibles for the role of his successor: R.A. Butler or Harold Macmillan. The Queen was asked to act as referee, and she chose Macmillan.

11   Eight: Churchill, Eden, Macmillan, Douglas-Home, Wilson, Heath, Callaghan and Mrs Thatcher.

12   Ian Smith – when Rhodesia issued its unilateral Declaration of Independence.

13   The red boxes contain documents that either require the Queen's signature, or else concern matters of which she should be aware. She spends the first hour or so of every day – wherever she may be – going through them.

14   No: and nor do Royal Dukes have votes.

Royalty and holidays

1 What Royal, when going on holiday abroad, always took a copper kettle on the journey – to ensure a decent cup of tea?

2 What Royal, prompted by an interest in horses, took a brief holiday at a house named Lane's End?

3 What Royal, on returning from a holiday abroad, helped to drive the Orient Express?

4 What Sovereign arrived at Naples escorted by eight battleships, four cruisers, and eight destroyers – and yet, on going ashore, travelled incognito?

5 What Royal said, 'Abroad is awful. I know because I've been there'?

6 What remote islands are visited annually by the Queen on her holiday?

7 When George V stayed at Bognor, it was to convalesce rather than to take a holiday. However, what object in the grounds of the house where he stayed must have reminded him of his grandmother?

8 Who takes the Queen's baggage when she goes on holiday – and what is its connection with the Charge of the Light Brigade?

9 When cruising in a steam yacht, a Royal suddenly realized that he/she was in love. Who?

10 When the Royal Yacht took the Prince and Princess of Wales on their honeymoon cruise, it departed from Gibraltar and eventually arrived at Port Said. Where, unknown to the rest of the world, did it call in between?

11 What Royal, on the eve of setting off on holiday, sat down to a dinner that included turtle soup, salmon steak, grilled chicken, a saddle of mutton, several snipe stuffed with foie gras, asparagus, a fruit dish, a large iced gateau, and a savoury?

12 Which Royal liked to travel to Le Touquet for a game of golf?

Answers   Royalty and holidays

1   Queen Victoria when travelling to the South of France.

2   Queen Elizabeth II. After a tour of Canada, she stayed for five days at Lane's End in Kentucky's Blue Grass country. Her host, oil millionaire Will Farish, is renowned for his collection of race horses.

3   Edward VIII. He was returning from Istanbul. As the great express passed through Bulgaria, King Boris (a keen railway buff) took over the controls of the locomotive. King Edward was invited to join him on the footplate, and was allowed to blow the whistle at approaches to level crossings.

4   King Edward VII.

5   King George V.

6   The Hebrides.

7   After his illness in 1929, George V stayed at Craigwell House, Bognor, to recuperate. The mainmast of one of Queen Victoria's steam yachts, *Elfin*, was hastily taken out of store (*Elfin* had long been scrapped), and erected in the grounds to serve as a flagstaff from which to fly the Royal Standard.

8   The Royal Baggage Train is provided by 20 Squadron of the Royal Transport Corps, and has its headquarters in Regent's Park Barracks, London. It was here that some sequences in *The Charge of the Light Brigade* (the version starring Trevor Howard as Cardigan) were filmed.

9   Edward VIII (then Prince of Wales) was cruising in Lord Moyne's yacht *Rosaura*, when he realized that he was in love with Mrs Simpson. The moment of revelation came after bad weather had forced the ship to put in at Corunna on the coast of Spain.

10   A Greek island.

11   Edward VII. His biographer, Sir Philip Magnus, records that he was seen 'to do full justice' to it. On the following day, the King set off for what was to be the last of many holidays spent at Biarritz.

12   King Edward VIII – as Prince of Wales.

Royalty and education

1   What Royal was employed as a housemaster at Wanganui Collegiate in New Zealand?

2   Which Sovereign founded Britain's second oldest public school – and what is the school?

3   Which Sovereign wanted his/her grandsons to be educated at a public school – i.e. Wellington College?

4   Which Royal incurred the wrath of his tutor by tricking him into eating a tadpole sandwich?

5   Who worked at the Young England Kindergarten?

6   Which Royal, commenting on his eldest son's educational progress, said that his 'intellect is of no more use than a pistol packed in the bottom of a trunk if one were attacked in the robber-invested Apennines'?

7   Who told a governess employed to tutor his grandchildren, 'For goodness sake teach . . . and . . . to write a decent hand, that's all I ask you. None of my children can write'. And what are the missing names?

8   Two Princesses were educated in Kent – who and where?

9   What was the culmination of Prince Charles's career at Gordonstoun?

10 How many 'O' and 'A' levels did Prince Andrew get?

11 In which College at what University was Prince Charles a student?

12 What degree did Prince Charles obtain?

13 What, in matters of education, did Captain Mark Phillips and the late Poet Laureate, Sir John Betjeman, have in common?

14 Where did Prince Andrew go after leaving Gordonstoun?

15 Who was the founder of a school attended by four members of the present Royal Family?

Answers   Royalty and education

1 Prince Edward.

2 Henry VI founded Eton in 1440. The oldest public school is Winchester College – founded in 1382.

3 Queen Victoria was anxious that Prince 'Eddy' and Prince George, the two sons of the Prince of Wales (Edward VII), should go to Wellington. Their parents opposed the idea, and won. The Princes went instead to the training establishment for future naval officers, HMS *Britannia*.

4 Edward VIII – when Prince of Wales.

5 The Princess of Wales.

6 Prince Albert was speaking of the future Edward VII.

7 King George V. The missing words are 'Margaret' and 'Lilibet' (Princess Elizabeth).

8 The Princess of Wales was educated at West Heath, near Sevenoaks, and Princess Anne at Benenden.

9 He was head of the school – or, in Gordonstoun parlance, 'Guardian'.

10 Prince Andrew did well: six 'O' Levels and three 'A' Levels. The Prince of Wales obtained two 'A' Levels – in history and French.

11 Trinity College, Cambridge.

12 A second class degree, which was not bad. It is thought that he might have done better, had not his official duties interrupted his studies.

13 Both went to the same public school – Marlborough.

14 Prince Andrew went to Lakefield College in Canada for six months – following the success of Prince Charles's sojourn at Timbertop in Australia. After that, he entered the Royal Navy.

15 The school is, of course, Gordonstoun, and the founder was Kurt Hahn. Just after the First World War, Hahn became headmaster of an establishment run on experimental lines at Salem in south Germany. Since he was born Jewish, he had to flee to Britain when the Nazis came to power. He was recuperating from an illness at a friend's house in Morayshire, when he spoke of his ambition to open a school in the UK run on the same principles as Salem. The Gordonstoun estate near Elgin was acquired, and Gordonstoun opened in the summer of 1934. Prince Philip, Prince Charles, Prince Andrew and Prince Edward were all educated there.

The reigns of Kings and Queens

1   What Sovereign in the history of British Monarchy had the longest reign?

2   Who lived to the greatest age?

3   The ancestry of the Queen can be traced back to William I. How many Sovereigns have there been in between?

4   Who was the youngest Sovereign ever to occupy the throne?

5   Who was Queen Jane?

6   Since 1066, four Sovereigns have occupied the throne for less than one year. Who were they?

7   For how long did the Prince Regent serve as such – and which King did he eventually become?

8   Who became heiress presumptive five times, and yet never succeeded to the throne?

9   Which two future Sovereigns were declared by Parliament to be illegitimate?

10 After the abdication of James II, three Stuarts claimed the throne of Britain. Had they been successful, what would have been their titles?

11 Who was the last entirely Welsh Prince of Wales?

12 Who was the most recent Sovereign whose father was never a reigning Monarch?

Answers The reigns of Kings and Queens

1   Queen Victoria. She reigned for 63 years.

2   Queen Victoria shares the distinction with George III. Both lived to be 81.

3   Forty.

4   Edward VI. He came to the throne at the age of nine, and died when he was sixteen.

5   Queen Jane was Lady Jane Grey, Edward VI's nominated successor. Nine days after her accession, she was deposed by Henry VIII's eldest daughter, Mary I. Queen Jane was beheaded at the tender age of seventeen.

6   Harold II (defeated by William I) reigned for only a matter of months. Edward V reigned for 75 days.* Queen Jane (already mentioned) sat on the throne for a brief nine days, and Edward VIII reigned for 325 days.

7   The future George IV was Prince Regent from 5 February 1811 until the death of his father, George III, in 1820.

8   Margaret Tudor. However, she did become Queen Consort of Scotland by her marriage to James IV. She was Henry VIII's sister.

9   Mary I and Elizabeth I: the former on the grounds of the alleged nullity of her parents' marriage (Henry VIII and Catherine of Aragon) – the latter because, said Parliament, Henry VIII and Anne Boleyn's marriage had to be considered invalid. However, both ladies had their own way when the Act of Succession was passed in 1544 and they were declared legitimate.

10   They would have been James III (sometimes known as 'The Old Pretender', and sometimes as 'The Old Chevalier'), Charles III (more commonly known as 'Bonny Prince Charlie'), and Henry IX (Prince Charlie's brother).

11   Llywelyn ap Gruffydd ap Llywelyn – or, to put it more succinctly, Llywelyn the Last. He died in 1282 during a skirmish with Edward I's knights.

12   Queen Victoria. Her father was Edward, Duke of Kent – the fourth son of George III.

*Edward V did not, in fact, reign at all. In 1483, the 13-year-old boy was confined to the Tower with his younger brother, the Duke of York – where the two were murdered. Richard III is generally assumed to have ordered the homicide, though the case is far from proven.

Royalty in sickness and in health

1 What Royal visited a 'pain healer' to remedy a shoulder injured while chopping logs at Balmoral?

2 Which Royal underwent an operation at Buckingham Palace, and consequently had to postpone an important engagement?

3 Which Sovereign underwent major surgery some months before he/she died – and what was the nature of the operation?

4 King George V went to Bognor to convalesce after a serious illness – what was that illness?

5 Which Royal helped to overcome the stress incurred by a long overseas tour by climbing a 300-ft cliff and then walking three miles?

6 What form of alternative medicine is used by the Royal Family?

7 Who keeps his/her throat clear by sucking cloves?

8 Back in history, two Sovereigns died from over-indulgence. Who were they – and in what did they over-indulge?

9 The Queen, apart from the usual complaints that everyone suffers, has one weakness. What is it?

10 What rare disease was transmitted by Queen Victoria?

11 What Sovereign's doctor became Auditor of the Duchy of Cornwall and Keeper of the Privy Purse?

12 What Sovereign's final illness began with a cold in the head?

13 What contribution to the nation's health was made by James I and the present Duke of Gloucester?

14 How many members of the medical profession belong to the Queen's Medical Household?

15 What famous author was cured of a serious complaint (or is said to have been) by a touch from his Sovereign's hand?

Answers   Royalty in sickness and in health

1   The Queen. On the recommendation of Princess Margaret, she attended Kay Kiernan's Bluestone Clinic in London's Marylebone Road. After two sessions on a pulsed high-frequency machine (known as PEME for 'pulsed electro magnetic energy'), the swelling and the pain disappeared.

2   King Edward VII was operated on for appendicitis. The postponed engagement was his coronation.

3   King George VI underwent an operation for lung resection – or, put more plainly, cancer. His death was caused by coronary thrombosis.

4   King George V's illness was pleuro-pneumonia. It was cured by draining off the fluid from an abscess on one of his lungs.

5   The Queen – after the Silver Jubilee tour of the Commonwealth in 1977. The cliff-climbing and the walk took place on Lundy Island.

6   Homoeopathy. Royalty's enthusiasm for this form of medicine dates back a number of years. On the day of King George V's funeral, the then physician to the Royal Family wrote out five prescriptions to be dispensed by Nelson's, the homoeopathic chemist, for three Kings and four Queens.

7   The Prince of Wales.

8   Henry I died of eating too many lampreys (a fish rather like an eel) in December 1135. In 1216, King John died at Newark after eating (or so it is said) too many peaches and drinking too much sweet ale.

9   Sinus trouble.

10   Haemophilia – or, as it is sometimes called, the bleeding disease, which is passed on by females and endured by males. It seems probable that Queen Victoria inherited the genes from her mother. Three of her daughters transmitted it; and, by their marriages, spread it through the Royal houses of Europe. Thus, via Princess Alice and then via Princess Alix (who married Nicholas II of Russia), haemophilia claimed its most famous victim – the young Tsarevich.

11   Sir William Knighton, a physician who had great influence over George III during that Monarch's declining years. Knighton attributed his success to his good bedside manner.

12   Queen Elizabeth I in 1603.

13   Both publicly opposed smoking – the Duke of Gloucester in a speech to the House of Lords; James I in his *Counterblast to Tobacco*, published anonymously in 1604.

14   Fourteen. They include the posts of Serjeant Surgeon and Physician to the Household.

15   At the age of two and a half, Dr Samuel Johnson suffered from scrofula (a tuberculous swelling of the lymphatic glands, which, for centuries, was known as the 'King's Evil', and could, it was claimed, be cured by the touch of the Sovereign's hand). Johnson was touched by Queen Anne – the last Monarch to practise the art. One has to assume that it was successful: he lived to the age of seventy-five.

Friends and connections

1   Which famous actress became a friend of the Prince of Wales (later Edward VII) when she was appearing at the Comédie Française in Paris?

2   Who, when a child, said to his/her playmate, 'I may call you Jane, but you must not call me . . . .'?

3   To whom were Prince Franz Joseph and Princess Gina of Lichtenstein host and hostess?

4   What friend of the Royal Family is always to be seen in the Royal box at the Albert Hall for the Festival of Remembrance?

5   What former King is godfather to Prince William?

6   To what overseas Sovereign did a British Monarch lend the Royal Yacht – with not entirely happy results?

7   With whom was a lady named Caroline Harbord-Hamond a school friend?

8   Who was Aunt Bessie?

9   What close friend of the Prince of Wales (later Edward VIII) fell out of favour when she went on a trip to America?

10 What friend of Edward VII was the grandfather of Edwina, Countess Mountbatten?

11 Which of Queen Victoria's Prime Ministers used to accompany her on her morning rides in Hyde Park?

12 Which actor played the part of his Royal friend in a film?

13 To whom was Lord Rupert Nevill a close friend as well as Private Secretary?

14 Lord and Lady Tryon are friends of the Prince of Wales. Where used the three of them to go for fishing holidays in the summer?

Answers   Friends and connections

1   Sarah Bernhardt. A rival, Lady Frederick Cavendish, described her as 'a woman of notorious, shameless character', which was grossly unfair.

2   Queen Victoria.

3   They entertained the Prince of Wales (later, the Princess of Wales as well) to skiing holidays. It was on one of them that the first major battle of the Princess versus the press photographers was fought. The Prince acted as peacemaker.

4   King Olaf of Norway.

5   King Constantine of the Hellenes.

6   Queen Victoria loaned the *Victoria and Albert* to the Empress of Austria for a trip from Britain to Madeira in 1860. The weather was vile, the Empress succumbed to seasickness, and it would have been better if she had chosen a shorter sea route.

7   Caroline Harbord-Hamond was friendly with Princess Diana when they were at school together at West Heath near Sevenoaks.

8   Aunt Bessie (or Bessie Merryman) was the Duchess of Windsor's aunt – and a considerable prop to her morale during the days of Edward VIII's Abdication.

9   Thelma, Lady Furness. During her visit to the United States, Mrs Simpson usurped her in the heart of the then Prince of Wales.

10   Sir Ernest Cassel, the multimillionaire banker who became the King's financial adviser.

11   Lord Melbourne. To the Queen, he was something of a father figure. As a private individual, his life was made immeasurably harder by his wife's (Lady Caroline Lamb) infatuation with the poet Byron – and her madness that probably resulted from it.

12   Noël Coward played the part of Lord Louis Mountbatten (later Earl Mountbatten of Burma) in the film *In Which We Serve,* based on Mountbatten's famous destroyer, HMS *Kelly.*

13   Lord Rupert Nevill was Prince Philip's Private Secretary and a close friend of both the Prince and the Queen. He has been described as almost a brother to Her Majesty.

14   The Prince used to accompany the Tryons to their lodge near Egilsstadir in Iceland for salmon fishing.

Maiden names

Who, before their marriages, were:

1 Baroness Marie-Christine von Reibnitz.

2 Lady Alice Montagu-Douglas-Scott.

3 Princess Marina of Greece and Denmark.

4 Katharine Worsley.

5 Lady Elizabeth Bowes-Lyon.

6 Princess Mary of Teck.

7 Edwina Ashley.

8 Wallis Warfield.

9 Charlotte of Mecklenburg-Strelitz.

10 Brigitte von Deurs.

11 Alexandra Princess of Denmark.

12 Victoria Alice Julie Marie Battenburg.

13 Victoria Princess of Saxe-Coburg.

14 Princess Victoria (Princess Royal).

Answers   Maiden names

1   Princess Michael of Kent.

2   The Dowager Duchess of Gloucester.

3   The late Duchess of Kent.

4   The present Duchess of Kent.

5   Queen Elizabeth – wife of George VI and the present Queen Mother.

6   Queen Mary – wife of George V.

7   Countess Mountbatten.

8   The Duchess of Windsor.

9   Queen Charlotte – wife of George III.

10   The Duchess of Gloucester.

11   Queen Alexandra – wife of Edward VII.

12   Princess Alice of Greece – mother of the Duke of Edinburgh.

13   The Duchess of Kent, Queen Victoria's mother.

14   Princess Victoria was Queen Victoria's eldest child. She married Prince Frederick of Prussia (later King Frederick III of Prussia) and gave birth to the future Kaiser Wilhelm II.

NOTE: the daughter of George V was also named Victoria and was the Princess Royal. She married the 6th Earl of Harewood.

Royalty and music

1 When was the National Anthem first performed?

2 Who, possibly, is the Queen's least favourite composer?

3 Who, conceiving a dislike for Handel's more sombre *Funeral March,* insisted that works by Beethoven and Chopin should be played at his/her funeral?

4 Which Sovereign was a prolific composer of music?

5 Which Master of the Queen's Music had, previously, composed the background music for a number of films – including a science fiction movie scripted by H.G. Wells?

6 What is a common factor of the last night of the Proms and a onetime Master of the King's Music?

7 Which Royal once delighted an audience by his rendering of the Pirate King in *The Pirates of Penzance*?

8 Which Royal is Patron and President of the Friends of the Royal Opera House at Covent Garden?

9 Which famous composer once entertained Queen Victoria by sitting at a piano and playing, simultaneously, the Austrian National Anthem with his left hand, and *Rule Britannia* with his right?

10 Which Royal could give passable renderings of the works of Beethoven, Debussy and Chopin by the age of 15?

11 Which Royal, when attending a recording session, evinced more interest in the equipment than in the music it was recording?

12 Which Royal is sometimes to be found at the piano, playing and singing Broadway melodies – with a cigarette in a jewelled holder in attendance?

13 Which Royal learned to play the bagpipes – an accomplishment that was not entirely pleasurable to his guests?

Answers   Royalty and music

1   *God Save the King/Queen* (by Thomas Arne who also wrote *Rule Britannia*) was first played at Drury Lane in 1745 – as a spontaneous expression of loyalty to George II during the Jacobite rebellion. It was first described as 'the National Anthem' in 1822.

2   Wagner might be a good bet. The Queen is known to dislike opera – and the works of Wagner in particular.

3   Queen Victoria. But she agreed that, now and then, a Highland lament might be allowed to intrude.

4   Henry VIII. Among his compositions were two five-part Masses, a motet (or anthem), and several instrumental pieces, part songs, and rounds.

5   Sir Arthur Bliss, who was Master of the Queen's Music from 1953 until 1975. The H.G. Wells film was *The Shape of Things to Come*.

6   The last night of the Proms reaches a kind of climax with *Land of Hope and Glory* composed by Sir Edward Elgar, who was Master of the King's music from 1924 to 1934.

7   Prince Charles – at Gordonstoun. The line 'Because with all our faults we love the Queen' was well applauded. Earlier, he had played one of the Dragoon Guards in *Patience*.

8   Prince Charles.

9   Mendelssohn.

10   The Queen.

11   Prince Philip.

12   Princess Margaret.

13   The Duke of Windsor – both as Prince of Wales and Edward VIII. He used to practise in the mornings on the terrace of his weekend retreat at Fort Belvedere.

Who said?

. . . or wrote the following:

1   The Lower Classes are becoming so well-informed – are so intelligent and earn their bread and riches so deservedly that they cannot and ought not to be kept back – to be abused by the wretched ignorant Highborn beings, who live only to kill time.

2   This morning, we have all become teetotallers until the end of the war. I have done it as an example, as there is a lot of drinking going on in the country.

3   Prince Philip is a born leader, but will need the exacting demands of a great service to do justice to himself. His best is outstanding; his second best is not good enough.

4   Things were done better in *my* day.

5   (Quoting from *The Desert* by Marine Louise Haskins) 'I said to the man who stood at the Gate of the Year, "Give me a light that I may tread safely into the unknown". And he replied, "Go out into the darkness and put your hand in the Hand of God. That shall be better than a light and safer than a known way" '.

6   What a pretty frock you are wearing.

7   I like to think I can go whenever I want to at short notice – turfing people out of the Royal Box so I can get a seat.

8   A custom loathsome to the eye, hateful to the nose, harmful to the brain, dangerous to the lungs, and in the black, stinking fume thereof, nearest resembling the horrible Stygian smoke of the pit that is bottomless.

9   Oh! he is mad is he? Then I wish he would *bite* some other of my generals.

10   Try sparrow-hawks, ma'am.

11   Who said, concerning whom, 'Get another electrician'?

Answers   Who said?

1   Queen Victoria to the Princess Royal in 1865. She felt that 'a new French Revolution' might be about to break out in England, and that the upper classes needed a severe shock before 'the dreadful crash'.

2   King George V. In 1915, British forces lost the Battle of Neuve Chapelle on the Western Front. The excuse of the general (Sir John French) was that his army ran short of shells. This was attributed to factory workers spending too much time in pubs, and not enough time making ammunition. When David Lloyd-George was appointed Minister of Munitions that June, he asked the King to set the nation an example. Hence what became known as the 'King's Pledge' was signed. After the war, His Majesty was able to enjoy a drink or two once more. But, for the general public, the effects of Neuve Chapelle survive to this day. As another measure, licensing hours were introduced: and they, unlike the King's Pledge, have not been rescinded.

3   Kurt Hahn, Headmaster of Gordonstoun, in his final report on Prince Philip.

4   Alice Keppel, the mistress of Edward VII, on the Abdication crisis.

5   King George VI. He used these lines at the end of his Christmas broadcast in 1939.

6   The Queen – to Maria Callas after a performance of *Tosca*. Somewhat lacking in enthusiasm for opera, Her Majesty seems to have been hard put to find something to say.

7   The Prince of Wales, remarking on the advantages of being Patron and President of the Friends of the Royal Opera House at Covent Garden.

8   James I. It is an extract from his *A Counterblast to Tobacco*.

9   King George II speaking of General Wolfe.

10   Advice from the Duke of Wellington to Queen Victoria when asked for a solution to the problems of the birds that were roosting in the trees within the Crystal Palace at the Great Exhibition of 1851.

11   Queen Victoria was referring to Guglielmo Marconi. She was staying at Osborne while the Prince of Wales was aboard the Royal Yacht off Cowes. Arrangements had been made to connect the two by wireless. Marconi was walking through the grounds of Osborne to inspect the aerial, when he was warned that he might disturb the Queen, who was taking a stroll. He refused to be diverted from his path – hence Her Majesty's remark.

Royalty and the Empire

1 Who was the first Royal to visit India – and when?

2 What army officer, who was involved with arrangements for a Royal tour of India, had a belt named after him?

3 What Sovereign (and when) rode on horseback to a gathering of Indian potentates – when some thought an elephant would have been a more appropriate mount?

4 Which Royal couple, when on passage to Canada, sailed over the spot where the *Titanic* had sunk – on, to quote one of them, *'just* about the same date!'?

5 What was the first passenger liner to do duty as a Royal Yacht on a tour of the Empire?

6 What male garment became popular as the result of a Royal tour?

7 Which Sovereign, on a visit to Nigeria, included a leper colony on the itinerary?

8 Which Royal, on riding to a gathering of army veterans in one of the Dominions, was pulled from the saddle and manhandled on to the rostrum?

9 What were known as 'the jewels of the Crown'?

10 Who, when a certain Prince visited India, turned up wearing diamonds worth £600,000 – and offered his guest six gold cannons valued at £40,000 apiece?

11 What went wrong when a Royal inaugurated the Australian Parliament at Melbourne in 1901?

12 What connection did a relative of the poet Rudyard Kipling have with India and the Royal residence at Osborne?

13 Who, and on what occasion, pressed a button in Buckingham Palace, and thus caused a message to be transmitted to the whole Empire?

14 On what overseas tour did the Gentlemen at Arms and the Royal Company of Archers attend the Sovereign?

15 On which tour were aircraft of the King's Flight first used?

Answers   Royalty and the Empire

1   The Prince of Wales (later Edward VII) visited India in 1875. The Queen had misgivings; Parliament was reluctant to pay for it; but the Prince had his way.

2   Sam Browne, who won the VC in the Indian Mutiny, was in charge of security arrangements for the Prince of Wales's 1875 visit.

3   King George V rode on horseback to his coronation durbar at Delhi in 1911. An elephant, it was thought, would have been a more prestigious mount.

4   King George VI and Queen Elizabeth on their journey to Canada and the United States in 1939. The Queen, who noted the coincidence, was slightly out in her dates. The *Titanic* sank on 15 April 1912. The *Empress of Australia* (in which the Royal party was travelling) passed over the spot in early May.

5   The Orient liner *Ophir* took the Prince and Princess of Wales (later King George V and Queen Mary) on a tour of the Far East in 1901.

6   The dinner jacket (or 'tuxedo') was worn by the Prince of Wales's all-male suite during his visit to India in 1875.

7   Queen Elizabeth II.

8   King Edward VIII when he was Prince of Wales. He was visiting a rally of 27,000 Canadian veterans at Toronto on Warriors' Day in 1919.

9   The colonies of the British Empire.

10   The twelve-year-old Gaekwar of Baroda. The Prince was unable to accept the cannons since they could not be regarded as ethnic products of Baroda.

11   The Princess of Wales pressed a button, which should have caused a Union Jack to be hauled to the masthead of every school in Australia. It did not work. (Canberra, incidentally, did not become the Australian capital until 1927.)

12   Kipling's father, who had been keeper of the museum at Mysore, designed the Durbar Room at Osborne, which reminded Queen Victoria of her possessions in India (but which she never visited).

13   Queen Victoria pressed the button before setting out on her Diamond Jubilee procession in 1897. It caused the central telegraph office in St Martin's le Grand to transmit: 'From my heart I thank my people. May God bless them'.

14   These two of the three Royal Bodyguards accompanied King George V and Queen Mary on their visit to India in 1911 – the year of their coronation. They made the voyage in the latest P&O liner, SS *Medina*.

15   On the Royal tour of South Africa in 1947/48, Vickers Vikings were used for some of the journeys.

Animals presented to Royalty

1   During a State Visit to Liberia in 1961, the Duke of Edinburgh was presented with two pygmy . . . . What?

2   In April 1956, Princess Anne was given an attractive creature named Nikki by the then Soviet leaders, Bulganin and Khrushchev. What was Nikki?

3   On what occasion did Prince Charles receive a dark brown stag named Goldie?

4   In October 1958, Prince Charles and Princess Anne were presented with a pair of small feathered companions named Annie and Davy. What were they?

5   Who was Harvey?

6   In May 1965 a nameless canary entered the Royal nursery. To whom was it given – and where was it born?

7   Aízita and Marquis are two oncas given to the Queen by the Mayor of Brasilia in 1968. What is an onca?

8   On the same State Visit to Brazil, the Queen received a mother and her baby. To what species did they belong? (Clue: guesswork would be idle.)

9   Mansa, who came from a sacred pond in a Gambian village, was a baby crocodile presented to Prince Edward in 1961. What does 'Mansa' mean?

10 Homing budgerigars seem to be at home on the terrace of what Royal residence?

11 Two beavers were given to the Sovereign by way of 'rent' by a large company operating in Canada. What is the company?

12 In March 1972, the Queen became the proud owner of two tortoises. Where was she when she received them?

13 What did the President of Cameroon send the Queen to mark her silver wedding in 1972? The name is 'Jumbo', which should be clue enough.

14 Who is Valentine? Who gave him to the Queen? And where does he live?

Answers Animals presented to Royalty

NOTE: Readers are reminded that death often gives no notice of its coming. Consequently, whilst the zoos in which some of these creatures live are mentioned, it cannot be guaranteed that the animals in question will be alive when this book is published.

1   Two pygmy hippopotami. The male died in 1967, but the female (Mary) survives at Whipsnade Zoo.

2   Nikki, now living in Regent's Park Zoo, is a brown Syrian bear – then three months old. Since then, he has sired four cubs with assistance from their mother, Winnie.

3   Goldie marked the 250th visitor under a reciprocal holiday exchange between Rapperswil in Switzerland and various London boroughs. He lived in the Regent's Park Zoo until his death in December 1965.

4   They were lovebirds presented by Mrs Audrey Pleydell Bouverie. One lived in the nursery and the other in the school room. After Annie (or was it Davy?) died, the survivor was given away.

5   Harvey was a white rabbit given to Prince Charles in 1953. For a while, he lived in the garden at Buckingham Palace. Then he was moved to the stables at Windsor where, in the summer of 1957, poor Harvey passed away.

6   The canary was given to the Queen after her State Visit to Germany in May 1965 – and so it seems fair to assume that this anonymous bird was born in Germany. Alas – its life was brief. It died in January of the following year.

7   An onca is a jaguar. Now they live in the Regent's Park Zoo.

8   Sloths. Unhappily, like the canary, they did not live to become old. They died at the Regent's Park Zoo shortly after their arrival at the end of 1968.

9   'Mansa' means King. The reign of this one was short. It is now dead.

10   On the terrace at Windsor.

11   The Hudsons Bay Company. The presentation was made at Winnipeg and the industrious little animals now live in the Regent's Park Zoo.

12   The tortoises were presented to the Queen when she visited the Seychelles. On coming to Britain, they took up residence in the Regent's Park Zoo.

13   'Jumbo', of course, is an elephant – a bull aged seven at the time. In 1973, he was transferred to Whipsnade, having lodged briefly at the GLC's Children's Zoo at Crystal Palace, and then at Regent's Park.

14   Valentine is a bay gelding – a gift from Queen Beatrix of the Netherlands on her State Visit to Britain in 1982. He now lives in the Royal Mews.

Royal routine

1 What is the first task undertaken by the Queen every day and no matter where she may be?

2 Who arranges the Queen's programme?

3 How far in advance are the movements of Prince Philip, Prince Charles, and Princess Anne, planned?

4 How many days a week does the Queen normally work when she is in residence at Buckingham Palace?

5 How does the Queen cope with jet lag?

6 Where do the Royal Family spend their summer holidays?

7 Where might you be likely to find the Queen (a) in January, and (b) in April?

8 Of what village is the Queen an active member of the Women's Institute?

9 Does the Queen carry money with her when she goes out?

10 How far in advance is a State Visit planned?

11 What is the Queen's taste in clothes for public occasions?

12 What small ceremony has the Prince of Wales gone on record as saying that the Queen performs more successfully than he?

1   Before doing anything else, the Queen studies the contents of the red dispatch boxes containing state documents.

2   Her Private Secretary. If the Queen cannot attend a particular event, he rings up the other private secretaries to see whether another member of the Royal Family can attend.

3   At the end of June and at the end of November, Prince Philip, Prince Charles, and Princess Anne – each of them holds a 'programme meeting'. Every invitation is studied and a schedule for the following six months is drawn up.

4   Four days – from Monday afternoon until Friday afternoon.

5   On the Queen's return to Britain after an overseas tour, her Private Secretary tries to keep a day or two clear of engagements. Similarly, when on tour, he tries to ensure that the first day is reasonably leisurely before the round of heavy duties begins.

6   At Balmoral – from mid-August until mid-October.

7   In January, at Sandringham; in April, at Windsor – though a visit overseas (e.g. to a meeting of the heads of Commonwealth Governments) may cause these interludes – and her summer holiday, too – to be cut short.

8   Sandringham's W.I.

9   No. By tradition, the Sovereign seldom carries any money. A Lady-in-Waiting is equipped with a supply of cash in case the Queen wishes to buy something.

10   A year at least – sometimes, two.

11   She likes lightish, brightish, colours for the very sensible reason that she can be seen more easily in them.

12   Planting ceremonial trees. Those planted by the Queen, it appears, do better than those planted by the Prince of Wales.

Royal pomp and heraldry

1 What symbol used to be erected in churches (and can still be seen in some) to demonstrate their loyalty to the Crown?

2 What is the meaning of Plantagenet?

3 What do three golden lions on a red shield symbolize – and who was the first Sovereign to use them?

4 What does the unicorn in the Royal Coat of Arms represent?

5 What Sovereign adopted the motto *Dieu et Mon Droit*?

6 Who formed the College of Arms, and who presides over it?

7 What used to be the duties of the Heralds?

8 What is a 'pursuivant'?

9 What was an early purpose of wearing a coat of arms?

10 In whose reign were the present Royal Arms introduced?

11 What part of the realm is not represented in the Royal Arms?

12 When was the ceremony of the Investiture of the Prince of Wales revived?

13 Who, until the coronation of William IV, used to lead the procession into Westminster Abbey?

14 At two coronations, the King's Champion got it wrong. Whose were they, and what was the trouble?

15 Who is the Garter King of Arms?

1   The Royal Coat of Arms.

2   Plantagenet is derived from *Planta Genista,* the Latin name for a sprig of broom that Henry II adopted as his emblem.

3   The three golden lions stand for England. Richard I was the first to use them.

4   The unicorn represents Scotland. James I of England (James VI of Scotland) introduced it.

5   Henry V – though Queen Elizabeth I and Queen Anne replaced it with *Semper Eadem* ('Always the Same').

6   The College of Arms, which is the ultimate authority on heraldry, was incorporated by a Royal Charter of Richard III. Its head is the Duke of Norfolk (the Earl Marshal), who nominates the Heralds for appointment by the Sovereign.

7   Until 1688, the Heralds toured the country – summoning all with claims to 'bear and use' arms to prove their entitlement.

8   A pursuivant is an Officer of the College of Arms below the rank of Herald.

9   The wearing of a coat of arms identified the leaders in a battle – just as a standard marked a rallying point.

10   In the reign of Queen Victoria.

11   Wales – it is regarded as a principality and not a nation (though Welsh nationalists would probably disagree).

12   Until 1617, the Prince of Wales and Earl of Chester was proclaimed in parliament at Westminster. This was discontinued to calm angry mutterings about Welsh nationalism. Queen Victoria, at the suggestion of the Bishop of Asaph, introduced the ceremony of investiture in Wales; Edward VII ignored it; and George V revived it.

13   The procession into the Abbey used to be led by the Royal Herb-Strewer, who strewed the carpet with 'Sweet Herbs and Flowers'. William IV stopped it on grounds of austerity. However, the Sovereign is still given a nosegay of sweet smelling flowers presented by the Worshipful Company of Gardeners.

14   At James II's coronation, the Champion climbed off his horse to kiss the King's hand – and fell over. His heavy armour made it difficult for him to regain his feet. At George III's coronation, the Champion's horse, which should make its exit from the ball backwards, mistook its instructions, and made its entry facing the wrong way.

15   The Garter King of Arms is the chief Herald in England, Wales and Northern Ireland. Among his responsibilities is that of attending to the affairs of the Noble Order of the Garter. He also introduces new peers into the House of Lords.

Royal monuments

1 A massive profile of a King, mounted on horseback, was carved on chalk downland – riding away from a seaside resort that he used to visit. Who was the King, and what was the resort?

2 A King, riding a charger, seems to stand guard outside the Palace of Westminster. Who is he?

3 Which King is immortalized outside which hospital – accompanied by statues depicting 'Lameness' and 'Sickness'?

4 How high is the Albert Memorial – and how long did it take to complete?

5 What do Charles I, George IV, Lord Nelson and Julius Caesar have in common?

6 Which Sovereign, known as 'the Sailor King', appropriately has his statue at Greenwich?

7 What do Queen Victoria and Peter Pan have in common?

8 Two Royals are remembered on the walls surrounding Marlborough House in London. Who are they?

9 Where can the Queen see a statue of her late father not far from her London home?

10 What Sovereign is commemorated at either end of a London thoroughfare?

11 What Sovereign, whilst criticizing the likeness of his/her late Consort, had to agree that the memorial in which it stood could 'be seen from a great distance'?

12 What Queen has a memorial in a station yard?

13 What Queen in distant history can be seen driving her chariot on the Thames Embankment?

14 In the grounds of Balmoral, there is a stone marking the place where . . . (who?) shot his last stag.

Answers   Royal monuments

1   George III on the downs near Weymouth. It is said that the King was displeased: the carving shows him riding away from the town. He would have preferred to be seen riding towards it.

2   Richard I. During the Second World War, the blast of a bomb bent the sword that Richard is brandishing – thus making him very nearly a figure of comedy. It has since been straightened.

3   Henry VIII – outside Saint Bartholomew's Hospital. It is the only statue of him in London. It seems unlikely that he would have enjoyed this association with illness, but he had no say in the matter. It was erected after his death.

4   The Albert Memorial is 175 feet high, and it took twenty years to complete. It was designed by Sir Gilbert Scott, who was also responsible for the hotel beside St Pancras Station in London.

5   Their memorials are all in, or close to, Trafalgar Square. Nelson's, of course, is the most imposing.

6   William IV.

7   Memorials to both are to be found in Kensington Gardens.

8   Queen Alexandra, widow of Edward VII, and Queen Mary, widow of George V. Marlborough House was the home of both, after the deaths of their respective husbands.

9   The Queen can see the statue of George VI whenever she drives along the Mall.

10   Admiralty Arch at one end of the Mall was built in 1911 as part of the national monument to Queen Victoria. At the other end, outside Buckingham Palace, there is another memorial to her.

11   Queen Victoria was referring to the Albert Memorial.

12   A monument to Queen Eleanor of Aquitaine (wife of Henry II and mother of Kings Richard I and John) stands in the yard of Charing Cross Station. The original was the thirteenth cross marking the progress of the dead Queen from Nottingham-shire to Westminster Abbey. The present edifice is not a copy: it was built in 1865 – two years after the station had been completed.

13   Queen Boadicea.

14   Prince Albert. Another stone commemorated his last shoot at Windsor. Queen Victoria caused innumerable memorials to be erected in remembrance of her 'dearest Albert' – despite, earlier in her reign, advice from her Prime Minister, Lord Melbourne, never to waste her money on such things.

Succession and precedence

1   What determines the order of succession to the British throne?

2   Why, whilst the Prince of Wales is Heir Apparent, was the Queen, when Princess Elizabeth, Heir Presumptive?

3   What can Prince Charles, his sons and brothers, attain that the Duke of Edinburgh can not?

4   Who is third in line to the throne?

5   What Royal was awakened in the middle of the night to be told that he/she had acceded to the throne?

6   Why, until comparatively recently, did Parliament have to be represented at the birth of a Royal child?

7   What Home Secretary spent two weeks kicking his heels in the Highlands, awaiting the birth of a Royal child?

8   Put the following in order of succession to the throne: Prince Edward, Princess Anne, Prince Andrew.

9   Prince Michael of Kent renounced his right to the throne when he became a Roman Catholic. Does this mean that his children, too, have to forgo it?

10 In order of precedence, who comes first: the Prince of Wales or Prince Philip?

11 In Scotland, the Duke of Rothesay ranks fourth in order of precedence. Who ranks above him – and who is the Duke of Rothesay?

12 Who, apart from the Sovereign, takes precedence: the Queen Mother or the Princess of Wales?

Answers   Succession and precedence

1 The Act of Settlement of 1701. Among other things, it insisted that the Sovereign must be a communicant of the Church of England.

2 Because, in matters of sovereignty, male heirs take precedence over female heirs. Thus Prince Charles is automatically heir to the throne; but, had King George VI produced a son, he would have become King – even though he would have been younger than the Princesses. (There was, of course, also the possibility that, while King, Edward VIII might yet marry and have children.)

3 The throne of Great Britain. The Duke of Edinburgh does not qualify.

4 The Prince and Princess of Wales's younger son, Prince Henry.

5 Queen Victoria. When the Archbishop of Canterbury, the Lord Chancellor, and the King's physician arrived at Kensington Palace after the death of William IV at Windsor, they had difficulty in summoning a servant to admit them.

6 It all had to do with the birth of James II's son in 1688 and the effort made to prevent his acceding to the throne. A scurrilous rumour was circulated that (despite more than enough witnesses) a Royal child had not been born, and that the baby was a changeling smuggled into the Queen's room in a warming-pan. To ensure that all was seen to be above-board in the future, Parliament insisted upon being represented at Royal births. The custom is no longer observed.

7 Sir William Joynson-Hicks arrived at Glamis Castle to witness the birth of Princess Margaret, but the Princess was a fortnight late in arriving.

8 Prince Andrew, Prince Edward, Princess Anne. Princess Anne is sixth in order of succession because she is a woman. It is a point upon which those who insist upon women's rights have yet to protest.

9 At present, the children of Prince and Princess Michael are eligible – providing they are brought up as Protestants. The Prince did not include any children he might have in his renunciation, which is why Pope Paul VI barred the couple from marrying in a Catholic church. However, the possibility is too remote to be worth serious consideration. Had he not married a Roman Catholic, Prince Michael would have been sixteenth in line to the throne.

10 Prince Philip. In a Royal Warrant dated 18 September 1952, it was declared that the Duke of Edinburgh should have precedence next to the Queen – and, consequently, before the Heir Apparent.

11 The Queen, the Duke of Edinburgh, and (when it is in session) the Lord High Commissioner to the General Assembly of the Church of Scotland. The Duke of Rothesay is better known as the Prince of Wales.

12 The Queen Mother takes precedence over the Princess of Wales – both in England and Scotland. The Queen's precedence is, of course, absolute.

When?

1 William of Normandy became King of England after winning the Battle of Hastings in 1066. What was the actual date of the battle?

2 On what date was Charles I executed?

3 On what date did Charles II return to England from exile in Holland?

4 George II breathed more easily after Prince Charles Stuart's Highlanders had been defeated at Culloden Moor. What was the date of the battle?

5 What occurred on 9 November 1841 that changed the date of a well-known ceremony?

6 What happy occasion was celebrated on 22 June 1897?

7 . . . and what sad event took place on 1 January 1901?

8 What important agreement, engineered by Edward VII, became a reality on 8 April 1904?

9 What was the date of Edward VIII's Abdication?

10 On what date do the Queen and Prince Philip celebrate their wedding anniversary?

11 Which Heir Apparent was born on 2 June in which year?

12 What important event in Prince Charles's life took place on 11 July 1969?

13 Which Royal was born on Christmas Day? And which King, long, long ago, was crowned on Christmas Day?

14 On what date did Queen Elizabeth accede to the throne?

15 Who married whom on 24 April 1963?

Answers When?

1 14 October 1066.

2 30 January 1649. There was snow on the ground.

3 25 May 1660.

4 16 April 1746.

5 The birth of the future Edward VII. As a result, Trooping the Colour was switched to a date in June and, thereafter, the Sovereign had an official as well as an actual birthday.

6 Queen Victoria's Diamond Jubilee.

7 Queen Victoria's death.

8 The Entente Cordiale between Britain and France.

9 10 December 1936.

10 20 November. The year of the Queen's marriage was 1947.

11 Prince William was born on 2 June 1982. He will not be Heir Apparent until his father comes to the throne; but this, hopefully, can be counted upon.

12 Prince Charles was invested as Prince of Wales at Caernarvon.

13 HRH Princess Alexandra was born on 25 December 1936. The Coronation of William I took place on it in 1066.

14 Immediately after the death of her father on 6 February 1952.

15 Princess Alexandra married the Hon. Angus Ogilvy, son of the 8th Earl of Airlie.